USA ELECTION-2020 ALL LIES!

WHY?
WHAT FOR?
WHAT ARE POSSIBLE SOLUTIONS?

USA ELECTION-2020 ALL LIES!

WHY?
WHAT FOR?
WHAT ARE POSSIBLE SOLUTIONS?

Dr. K. Anayet

About The Book

In this book you will learn about USA Election 2020 campaign stage and elect the President of the United States of America?

It is a great story of attacking, insulting, blaming, pounding, pressing, hammering, polite religious cheating, back biting, hating, and dividing. Wonderful journey, it is totally unbelievable in American history! It is nothing but all about lying!

This chapbook tells you what possible solutions you have, to control this corrupted world and how to get rid of all abnormal activities from our modern society today? I have written **23** best solutions for this corrupted G20 world leaders to avoid global conflicts and unrest if they follow on it. Disseminate this message to this world reader if you wish right away.

You will learn some advice written to US President, its advisory group, Pastors and G7, G8, G20 leader's advisory group. You will see whether they are really doing their job or not? I believe the role of advisory group has tremendous effects of Presidents decision, what to say and what not to say, what to do and what not to do and finally stay in peaceful positive reliable safe position. It is a great issue for this corrupted world, **we are on top of fire**.

You will also learn who is fueling to make this world unrest and making the global environment toxic, bitter smelly and unpleasant. I have written **18** major systemic injustices happening around this world. My intention is not to increase the page numbers; I focused on the relevant information about USA Election-2020.

I am criticizing both parties from the neutral point of view for best outcome and striking the main point instead of working on the periphery of a circle.

I am not focusing who will win in this upcoming election. I am trying to explore the truth and tell the truth to the public and let the world know about this truth. My focus not care who will win in this 2020 election that is not my purpose.

Contents written in this chapbook based on:

- **Democratic & Republican Party** backgrounds, philosophy, principles, ideology, vision, ethics, and how they are working with China, Russia, France, United Kingdom, Germany and playing the blaming game and make the whole world unrest. As a result, the environment becomes toxic, bitter, smelly and unpleasant. They also play with United Nations (UN), NATO to control and impose sanctions on other countries and so on,

I used very simple English in this book so that everybody can understand without going to find the word meaning in dictionary or search engine like Google.

Dr. K. Anayet

Dedication

This book is dedicated to specific readers who are they? They are USA based leaders including G7, G8 and G20 country top leaders in the world.

List of Abbreviations

BG	Bill Gates
COVID-19	Corona Virus Disease-2019
PM	Prime Minster
R&D	Research and Development
USA	United States of America
UN	United Nations
UNSC	United Nations Security Council
WHO	World Health Organization

Contents

Acknowledgments..1
Introduction...2
CHAPTER 1..13
   USA Election-2020 Features............................13
   What USA Election-2020 Brought Back to Us!
....13
   Author's Opinion...27
CHAPTER 2..30
   Injustice Happening Around The World..........30
   1: USA Election-2020 Nights...........................33
   2: George Floyd Killing! May-2020.................35
   3: Jacob Blake Killing! August-2020................38
   4: Portland Killing! August-2020.....................41
   5: Drive Through on Crowd in Portland!
August-2020...43
   6: Israel & UAE Peace Agreement...................45
   What is happening in Kashmir, India &
Pakistan?..47
   7: Israel & Palestine Conflicts.........................48
   8: Who is Biggest Pollution Maker?................50
   9: Ministry Allocation In Ontario.....................51
   10: Bill 21 In Ontario......................................54
   11: Worldwide Muslim is a Terrorist-How?...57
   12: France Teacher Beheaded-How?................59
   13: G7, G8 and G20 Country Top Leaders.....65
   14: Spiritual Worlds...74
   15: Technological Advancement Worlds........75
   16: Bill Gates Outstanding Speech...................78
   17: Own House/Family....................................82

18: Local Community/Neighborhood..............83
19: Workplace..85
Problems Can Be Solved Within One (1) Minute But It Takes Long Time.......................90
Summary From All Above Systemic Injustice Scenario...91
Dear G7, G8 & G20 Country Top Leaders.....94
CHAPTER 3..96
Advice To US President & His Advisory Groups..96
1: Advice goes to Mr. US President................97
2: Advice goes to Advisory Group................100
Few Questions Mr. Advisor...........................105
3: Advice goes to Mr. Pastor..........................108
Few Questions Mr. Pastor..............................109
4: Advice Goes To G7, G8 & G20 Country Top Leaders...112
Few Questions Respective Advisors of G20 Countries Top Leaders....................................117
CHAPTER 4..118
The Best Solution For United States Of America (USA) & Rest Of The World!........118
Democratic Party In USA..............................119
Republican Party (GOP) In USA..................121
The Summary From Both Republican & Democratic Parties..123
Thinking For Best Solutions!.........................124
How Does It Work?.......................................126
Share My Idea With Justice Systems............128
Solutions For USA & Rest Of The World.....129
Slogan For 21st Century!...............................150
Call For Global Peace Conference................152
REFERENCES..154

From Al-Quran..................................154
From Websites.................................154
ABOUT THE AUTHOR...................................156
GLOSSARY...157

Acknowledgments

All the praise is due to God for the opportunity and the strength He gave me to study, doing research and write-up towards this chapbook.

I express my gratefulness to my wife and children because they helped me a lot to finish this book.

I would like to extend my appreciation to my relatives, friends, neighbors, co-workers and other community members, people from different religion such as Pastor, Priest, Rabbi, Imam, Shiekh and they are my royal fans and best advocates for this chapbook, I really appreciate for their role and activities what I have learned from them.

Introduction

I was thinking during write-up this chapbook that I should study Law or International Politics instead of Electrical & Power Engineering. I felt slight regret for that because the current **corrupted** world is so brutal, crucial and many people do not want to write-up about the truth.

I was watching you tubes, newspapers, national convention, presidential debates, election night and online sources to monitor USA election-2020 campaign stage and final results.

I found it is a questionable election on this planet compared to third world countries. I was thinking what they (the rest of the world) will learn from this election?

It is an offensive, disgraceful and extreme racial conflict in the history of United States of America as per my tiny knowledge. Again, you might say that you are 100% correct, I am not arguing with you.

New York City does not welcome US president to do pre-election campaign to visit the city. Similarly, Kenosha City does not welcome US President to visit the city, and Nevada as well. So there is a big question mark, why?

I was thinking US President will resign or withdrawn his candidacy from this 2020 election after clash on the streets and will make history and the whole world will salute him for his extraordinary decision, but who cares this world?

They applied "might is right or tit-for-tat" principle during their pre-election campaign time, it is similar pattern what I found compared with in South Asia and their main goal how to win in the election and get the governmental power.

What I am trying say in South Asia, they do not care what other people said to them, they always applied "might is right or tit-for-tat" principle during their election time, their main goal how to win in the election.

- They are super greedy,
- They are super hungry for governmental power,

Similarly, in USA election-2020, I saw almost same principle they applied, they do not care what the rest of the world said, they applied "might is right or tit-for-tat" principle during their election time, it is similar pattern with Asia that main goal how to win in the election.

Currently, USA is leading the whole world (as of November 2020) and administering and liaising with other countries to monitor and maintain leadership activities.

But they are doing in their pre-election campaign stage sort of autocratic behavior,

For examples,
- It is a great story of attacking, insulting, blaming, pounding, pressing, hammering, religious polite cheating, back biting, hating, and dividing,
- It is all about lying and achieved their personal desire or goals!

- It is all about prides, let the world know "Who am I?" "I have a lot of power" "I can do whatever I like" as US President, I can do that, I can do this etc.,

I am not focusing who will win in this upcoming election. I am trying to explore the truth and tell the truth to the public and let the world know about this truth. My focus not care who will win in this 2020 election that is not my purpose.

This chapbook tells you what possible solutions to control this **corrupted** world are and how to get rid of all abnormal activities from our modern society today? Disseminate this message to this world reader if you wish right away.

I have read many books written by many famous reporters worldwide, many intellectuals, but nobody propose solutions, how to solve the current problems in this world, everybody writing up their book 600 pages or 1000 pages and getting best seller award. I do not understand why not writing about problems and its solutions, and ask every nation to come forward and solve the problem what we have now.

In this chapbook, I have criticized the Republican and Democratic leadership including G7, G8 and G20 country top leaders.

My intention is not to hurt any individual. I solely criticize the systems and decision making mechanism, who run this society so that we all together can be improved and as a result, will enjoy the better healthy life in this world instead of an epidemic or pandemic.

If someone is hurt after reading my chapbook, please forgive me from your heart, again this is not my intention to hurt you at individual level. I believe in <u>positive criticism</u> on everything in this universe and this can improve the leadership control systems.

This book is about to find out who creates problem in our modern society and how to get rid of those problems. My intention striking to the main point and not wasting time for readers to read up 600 or 1000 more pages, I wrote briefly in this chapbook the main concerns of systemic injustice and its solutions based on my personal views.

To understand my criticism I would request every reader that please read **Chapter 1** where I have written sort of election features and what USA Election-2020 taught and brought back to us! It is a great story of attacking, insulting, blaming, pounding, pressing, hammering, religious cheating, back biting, hating, and dividing. Wonderful journey, it is totally unbelievable in American history! It is nothing but all about lying and priding!

They do not talk about general ethics, work ethics, family ethics, community ethics, morality and how it will be implemented in our people's mind of modern society.

Then I would request to read **Chapter 2** where I wrote something about 18 "systemic injustice". I discussed briefly about systemic injustice and systemic racism occurred during 2020 pre-election stage in United States of America (USA). Also it has been discussed briefly about systemic injustice and systemic racism happening worldwide. Please have a look.

I found systemic injustice exist every corner of our modern society that really influenced me to write-up about this Chapbook,

I found US President, G7, G8 and G20 country top leaders do not have enough time to look after what kind of systemic injustice happening worldwide, they always super busy with "ego & pride" and what else I am not sure. I found G7, G8 and G20 country top leaders do not have enough time to study about what is "positive criticism" and what it can do?

They do not accept positive criticism and as a result, they misunderstood and blaming each other country. Even they do not trust each other country,

- as a result, the ultimate goal of the world becomes very **toxic, bitter, unpleasant, smelly, suspicious** and **politically unrest**.

Then I would request to read **Chapter 4** where I wrote something about 23 solutions to avoid current conflicts in this world. In this chapter, I discussed some sort of solutions for United States of America (USA) where both parties face tremendous abnormal pressure during their 2020 pre-election time. Also it has been discussed briefly some solutions for the rest of the world. Please have a look!

The solution I propose here that might be works for you or might not be work but at least my positive efforts are there based on my tiny knowledge; the decision is yours, what to do and what not to do. My job is to tell you, the rest is yours.

Then I would request to go through **Chapter 3** where I wrote some advice and asking for their opinion to US President and his advisory groups. In this chapter, I have discussed briefly about the duty of "advisory group" of US President and advisor of G7, G8, G20 leaders.

I believe the role of advisory group has tremendous effects of Presidents decision, what to say and what not to say, what to do and what not to do and finally stay in peaceful positive position. I guess the advisory group did not advise their President how to bring people together and unite them and move forward.

At the end, I would like to say that try to understand the facts from your heart before the earth discharges its burdens [99:2].

To get rid of all kinds of conflicts from our modern society, we have to act now together positively before the earth discharges its burdens [99:2], so we need to know how to do that and what to do to avoid Global conflict and unrest?

If you don't like it, then you may ignore it. If you like it, go ahead; carry on my world on this planet.

Finally, I would say, I am grateful to all of you that you have decided to read this book.

I believe that you will get some positive motivation towards building a healthy community or society after reading this chapbook by the grace of Almighty God.

CHAPTER 1

USA Election-2020 Features

In this chapter, I have discussed some features or characteristics what USA election-2020 taught and brought back to us and what we have learned or the rest of the world has learned from this election. I am just sharing my ideas; the decision is yours, what to do and what not to do. My job is to tell you, the rest is yours.

What USA Election-2020 Brought Back to Us!

- USA Election-2020 taught us how to **attack** the opponent or opposition party and vice-versa,

- USA Election-2020 taught us how to **insult** the opponent or opposition party and vice-versa,

- USA Election-2020 taught us how to **blame** the opponent or opposition party and vice-versa,

- USA Election-2020 taught us how to **pounding, pressing and hammering** the opponent or opposition party and vice-versa,

- USA Election-2020 taught us how to **back bites** about opponent or opposition party and vice-versa,

- USA Election-2020 taught us how to behave as **egotistic or pride** way to the opponent or opposition party and vice-versa,

- USA Election-2020 taught us how to **hate** the opponent or opposition party and vice-versa,

- USA Election-2020 taught us how to **divide** the nation and **no respect** towards American people from the bottom of the heart, to desire the personal goal based on politics and vice-versa,

- USA Election-2020 taught us how to build **white supremacy** among American people and make a general conflicts among themselves like **White 2 Black & Rich 2 Poor** and so on,

- USA Election-2020 taught us how to "**tell a lie**" to the public meeting, national convention and on election night about opponent or opposition party and vice-versa,

- USA Election-2020 taught us how to "**do a plotting**" with opponent or opposition party, US President said during election night-2020, after 4am if "mail in vote" counts, then we will go to court, this is a major fraud in our nation, we want the Law to be used in proper manner, we do not want to add ballots in the list after 4am, wonderful US President, it is unbelievable in American history of politics. I believe the whole world watching and become a full of fool to listen this statement by US President,

- USA Election-2020 taught us how to **do religious polite cheating** with the general public and/or opposition party and vice-versa using religious Pastor or evangelist,

- USA Election-2020 taught us how to "**show up or pride**" to the public that "I have this, I am a big guy, I can do this, I can deploy, I can do everything" and so on. Everything around "I" not "We", there is nobody except I, I am the one can do everything; I can "Make America Great Again"!

- Trump campaign **sues** to stop vote counting in 2 states as Biden wins 2 key battlegrounds states, as vote counting continues, here are the **lawsuits** Trump has filed,

- Trump suggests he might **fire** Dr Fauci after election CNN.com, how it is possible for US President saying non-sense statement,

On top of the above phenomena, there are some funny and practical blaming games are listed below for world readers:

First, I will discuss briefly about **Kamala Harris** chosen for Vice-President Candidate of the United States of America under Democratic Party.

Kamala Devi Harris born October 20, 1964 is an American politician and lawyer who has served as the junior United States Senator from California since 2017.

She is the Democratic Presidential Nominee for the 2020 election. Born in Oakland, California, Harris graduated from Howard University and the University of California, Hasting College of the Law.

This is absolutely Democratic Party's own concern to whom they will give nominee for 2020 election as Vise-President of the United States of America.

She began her career in the Alameda County District Attorney's Office, before being recruited to the San Francisco District Attorney's Office and later the City Attorney of San Francisco's office.

There is nothing much concern for the Republican Party about Kamala Harris because she is selected by Democratic Party.

But Republican Party leader made a very nasty comment about Kamala Harris as listed below:

- KAMALA HARRIS is a "Nasty women",

- KAMALA HARRIS is an "Angry women",

- KAMALA HARRIS is a "Racial women",

- KAMALA HARRIS is a "Mad women",

WOW!

President of the United States of America ramps up attacks on Kamala Harris!

- What kind of message President gave the world using this comments,
- The rest of the world what will learn from this behavior,

My intention is to explore the truth and tell the truth to the public and let the world know about this truth.

My focus not care who will win in this 2020 election, that is not my purpose,

Second, I will discuss briefly about **post office mailing scandal.** I am not why US President not agreeing to adopt mail-in-ballots, but it seems doubtful.

I am writing-up a little heads-up from US President as follows:

Mail-in ballots a disaster: Trump

In his closing statement, Trump has reiterated that mail-in ballots "is a disaster".

"This is going to be a fraud like you have never seen. We are going to do well. But, who knows? We are not going to know (the election results) for months."

So let the world think about this!

Third, I will discuss briefly about New York City why not welcoming the President of The United States to visit the city,

It is big question for the rest of the world, why?

It is declared by NY city governor Andrew Cuomo,

I am writing some comments directly from Cuomo as follows:

- CUOMO tells Trump He's not welcome in New York City,

- "Look, the best thing he did for New York City was leave. Good riddance let him go to Florida, be careful not to get COVID…,

- COVID ambushed New York due to Trump's negligence… He is the cause of COVID in New York,

- Changed his residence to go to Florida, Why?

- He can't come back to New York. He can't,

- He's going to walk down the street in New York?

- Forget bodyguards he better have an army if he think he's going to walk down the street in New York…

- No, New Yorkers don't want to have anything to do with him and he knows it".

Can you imagine the level of systemic injustice where it is now?

It is totally out of control, boiling now; it becomes a toxic, bitter and unpleasant smell.

I do not know how to explain this injustice, it is unbelievable!

Fourth, I will discuss briefly about Kenosha City why not welcoming the President of The United States to visit the city,

What does it mean?

It is declared by Kenosha city mayor John Antaramian.

Can you imagine the level of systemic injustice where it is now?

It is totally out of control, boiling now; it becomes a toxic, bitter and unpleasant smell.

I do not know how to explain this injustice, it is unbelievable!

Fifth, I will discuss briefly about COVID-19 which is still going on during these pre-election campaign stage (January-November) and what they are doing for public.

People already know about this COVID-19 still no vaccine declare yet except Russia.

We are not in a position of 100% to reopen, still fighting with COVID-19 viruses.

The "Day Cares, Elementary School, Colleges and Universities" all are online working remotely but surprisingly both parties are making a playing game with COVID-19 all over.

Wonderful! Carry on USA!

We are still fighting with these unseen viruses and everyday people are dying.

I am sharing the statistics from WORLDOMETER for my world readers.

The statistics says as per "worldometer" as of **August 30, 2020** in USA,

- Total cases 6,173,236,
- Total deaths 187,224 and
- Total recovered 3,425,723.

Again, just for comparison for 5 Days,

The statistics says as per "worldometer" as of **September 3, 2020** in USA,

- Total cases 6,335,224,
- Total deaths 191,058 and
- Total recovered 3,575,096,

During these 5 Days TOTAL DEATHS found in USA are 3834 people,

This is just very simple example that during 5 days total 3834 people died and they do not care about this, who are they?

- They are great American Politicians!

- WOW! Really great!

- The whole world will remember them, fantastic!

My intention is to explore the truth and tell the truth to the public and let the world know about this truth.

I do not care who will win in this 2020 election, that is not my purpose,

Furthermore,

The statistics says as per "worldometer" as of **October 30, 2020** in USA,

- Total cases 9,212,767,
- Total deaths 234,177 and
- Total recovered 5,983,345,

During these 61 Days TOTAL DEATHS found in USA are <u>46,933</u> people [<u>Forty Six Thousands Nine Hundreds Thirty Three People Passed Away</u>],

3 days left for November 3, 2020 (Election Day]

WHO warns that please maintain social distancing and wearing mask that will reduce the contamination and overall death rates,

WHO also says 50,000 people died each week!

Who cares?

Democratic and Republican parties, they do not have time to listen because they have to win for USA Election-2020!

For What!

To Make America Great Again!

Not for American People, let them die by COVID-19, it does not matter!

Finally, this is a great lesson what USA Election-2020 brought back to us for this current **corrupted** world for those who are wise and intelligent enough otherwise the current world will be unrest and the environment would be bitter and toxic and it will remain unrest, toxic and bitter, nobody can change it.

I am pretty much doubtful that it will remain there!

Think for a Minute:

- Why we are **attacking** each other?
-
- Why we are **insulting** each other?
- Why we are **blaming** each other?
- Why we are so **egotistic** each other?
- Why we are **back biting** each other?
- Why we are **pounding**, **hammering** and **pressing** each other?
- Democratic and Republican convention deliver whirlwind of **lies** great and small, what does it mean?

It means that there is something shortage! There is something missing!

What is that?

What is the missing component?

The name of that missing component is as listed below:

- **Justice**,
- **Peace**,
- **Gratefulness**,
- **Humbleness** and so on,

The above all types of conflicts (**attacking, insulting, blaming, back biting, pressing, pounding, hammering** etc.,) can be solved within short period of time,

- if our G7, G8, G20 country top leaders accept **positive criticism, positive attitudes**,
- if our G7, G8, and G20 country top leaders have minimum **spiritual knowledge**,
- and if G7, G8, and G20 country top leaders they practice **moral facts** in their real life,
- and if G7, G8, and G20 country top leaders they maintain minimum spiritual knowledge in their personal life,

As a result, 7 billion people of the world can breathe in and out peacefully fresh breath. We need fresh breath in & out,

- <u>We are on top of fire</u>.

Author's Opinion

If you think that I am writing wrong information in this Chapbook and then you guys penalize me. I will accept your penalty but in return, I would like to get the following positive commitments from you for this world:

- I want this world to be safe and reliable to live so that all human being can live and walk around peacefully, love each other positively in a racism free society,

- I want calm and quite peaceful world, no blaming game among G7, G8 & G20 countries, no sanction from G7 country top leaders to underdeveloped countries without valid justification,

- I want USA to disclose what happen in China about COVID-19 as US president claimed that China knows in this regard,

- I want the USA will disclose the real facts that who attacked Twin Towers in Sep 11, 2001 and let the world know the real facts and penalize the real criminals/culprits openly in front of 7 billion people so that every people in this world can learn from this incident rather blaming and making nasty politics throughout the world,

- I want United Nations (UN) will function properly without interruption so that every independent country can exercise their full rights,

- I want United Nations (UN), G20 country top leaders and UN Veto Power Countries (all 5) will take strong initiatives to solve the problems/systemic injustice happening to following issues:

  - Conflicts between Palestine and Israel,
  - Conflicts between Kashmir, Pakistan and India,
  - Conflicts in Myanmar killing Muslims and pushing back to Bangladesh,
  - Injustice happening in China Uyghur Muslim community against humanity,
  - Conflicts between Syria, Iraq, Iran, Armenia, Azerbaijan, Afghan and so on,

- I want no war, no biological warfare, no nuclear war, no dispute for this world, should be absolutely free perfect world,

- I want justice/peace everywhere in this world (The current world is a full of systemic injustice-see Chapter 2 for details),

- I don't want to see the world again like the year 1720, 1820, 1920, 2020 where parents lost their loved ones and vice-versa,

I strongly believe that G7, G8 and G20 country top leaders including top 50 richest people can change this world if they accept positive criticism from the bottom of their heart due to the following reasons:

- Because they are the one, who is controlling the business worldwide and making the world politically unrest,
- Brainwashing the teenage people's mind,
- Controlling the print media,
- Controlling the underground world,
- At a glance, controlling everything in this world.

- Therefore, my blame goes to them, simultaneously my thanks also goes to them for doing partially good thing in this world!

The above all types of conflicts can be solved within short period of time if they accept **positive** criticism. As a result, 7 billion people can breathe in and out peacefully.

We are on top of fire.

To get rid of all kinds of conflicts from our modern society, we have to act now before the earth discharges its burdens [99:2], so we need to know how to do that and what are the process involve to do that?

Let's see the next topics how systemic injustice happening around the world/globe.

CHAPTER 2

Injustice Happening Around The World

In this chapter, I have discussed briefly about systemic injustice and systemic racism occurred during 2020 pre-election stage in United States of America (USA). Also I will discuss briefly about systemic injustice and systemic racism happening worldwide. Please have a look!

Few Examples of Major Injustice Happened During 2020-Election in USA:

- **George Floyd killings** happened on May 25, 2020 (Monday) in USA while pandemic COVID-19 is still going on and police officer killed him in front of public,

- **Jacob Blake killings** and he was shot 7 times in front of his 3 children during daylight by Kenosha, Wisconsin Police Officer,

- Trump trade blame after fatal protest shooting, **1 man dead** after groups clashed in the city's streets Saturday night in Portland, Oregon on August 29, 2020,

- Trump supporters **drive through** on crowd and pepper spray protesters in **Portland**, Oregon, the whole world has seen those scenarios, it is unbelievable!
- **Media** is divided in two (2) main streams, in my eyes. Republican media, for example, HANNITY, FOX NEWS they are little bit inclined to Republican, I might be wrong but this is views towards them, similarly, Democratic media, for example, CNN, MSNBC, what does it mean? This is a problem for our modern society, this is called systemic injustice which is already entered or penetrated the local administration. All news media should work how to "Make America Great Again".

- **New York** (NY) city not welcoming US president to visit them, it is big question for the rest of the world, why? It is declared by NY city governor Andrew Cuomo, what does it mean? Can you imagine the level of systemic injustice where it is now? It is totally out of control, boiling now; it becomes a toxic, bitter and unpleasant smell. I do not know how to explain this injustice, it is unbelievable!

- Similarly, **Konosha city** not welcoming US president to visit them during US election pre-campaign stage, what does it mean? It is declared by Kenosha city mayor John Antaramian. Can you imagine the level of systemic injustice where it is now? It is totally out of control, boiling now; it becomes a toxic, bitter and unpleasant smell. I do not know how to explain this injustice, it is unbelievable!

- Trump faces backlash for urging people to vote twice to test mail in ballot system,

- It is very crystal clear that both Republican and Democratic parties are **blaming, attacking, insulting, lying, back biting, pressing, pounding, hammering, stealing, hating, dividing and religious cheating** 100% each other, no doubt, the level of blaming and attacking is almost out of control,

- It is something like "rich people" always pressing or pounding on "poor people" what I have seen in South Asia, now watching in North America, wonderful! Carry on USA!

- It seems "Republican" become rich and pressing "Democratic Party" and the next "Democratic" become rich and pressing "Republican Party" and vice-versa,

Other Than Above, Now Back To The Main Point For Details How Systemic Injustice Happening Around The United States Of America (USA) And Globally,

Please have a look below for details,

1: USA Election-2020 Nights

US President made a fake story during election-2020 nights and has filed lawsuits against opposition party saying that stealing votes, ballots whereas still he is (Donald Trump) in power, even without proper evidence how US President can claim that stealing votes, it is simply unbelievable in American history of politics,

That is simply wrong, I would say "lawsuits" against democracy at these circumstances, it is a huge injustice in my eyes and we are on top of fire! Democracy is questionable in USA!

I saw on You Tubes the Trump's lawyer's conversation and his face while he was speaking, I found him that he was trying to convince the people saying that ballots has been taken away or some sort of blaming against opposition party.

I would say that we (as highly educated people) damaging this world and making the environment toxic, bitter, unpleasant and smelly (**like skunk smell**-very hard to stay there),

For examples,

This lawyer is sold out by Trump associates, I guess, I might be wrong but this is my personal views,

What does it mean? It means that this gentleman is qualified and educated, he is working for Trump, where is **work ethics**? The whole world knows that this is not a legitimate issue, it is man-made issue, similar to COVID-19 which is called China Virus, it means man-made.

Trump said "Joe Biden" is the worst Presidential candidate in the American history of politics, what is non-sense talking as US President and people around him clapping and encouraging, what a wonderful talk! If he loses with Biden, then he might leave the country!

It seems USA is following South Asian countries, if ruling party fails in election, then they start claiming that election has been stolen by opposition party, same thing happen in USA Election-2020, Wonderful!

The people came out on the road during post-election-2020 in NY Manhattan, Portland, California and Chicago saying we want our human rights and so on. The rest of the world respect USA because they follows some certain standards for democracy and legal systems, but this time in USA Election-2020 what happened to them?

However, in my eyes, it is an offensive, disgraceful and extreme racial election campaign and post-operative election activities in the American history of politics.

It is full of injustice in our modern society, with my tiny brain I don't know why?

- Time to rethink! Time to reform!

2: George Floyd Killing! May-2020

George Perry Floyd Jr. was an African-American man killed during an arrest after a store clerk alleged he had passed a counterfeit $20 bill in Minneapolis.

A white police officer named Derek Chauvin knelt on Floyd's neck for a period initially reported to be 8 minutes and 46 seconds.

Believe me I was so emotional after watching the youtube and momentarily I lost my breath to talk with my friend, I told him wait please I can't talk.

I believe this incident happened on May 25, 2020 (Monday) in USA while pandemic is still going on and police officer killed him in front of public. It is unbelievable!

I am writing up some of the conversations between Floyd and police officer:

- Floyd can be heard saying in the video: "Please, please, I cannot breathe."
- The officer tells Floyd to "relax".
- Floyd responds: "I can't breathe. Please, the knee in my neck".
- The officer continues to hold down Floyd with his knee for several minutes, with Floyd pleading and asking for **water**.
- "My stomach hurts. My neck hurts. Please, please. I can't breathe," Floyd cries out, while moaning and trying to cough.

Floyd eventually appears motionless under the officer's knee. Those who were watching the incident unfold can be heard begging police to move off Floyd.

So I am hopeless, I don't know what to say here.

- Where is justice?
- Where is my peace?
- I lost my language to talk!
- I am asking you where is solidarity in USA whereas **Republican** said in their Republican National Convention-2020 (RNC Day#1) that America is a "Land of Promised"!

It is offensive, disgraceful and extreme racial conflict in the United States of America.

I am here to condemn!

The whole world is condemning against this racial brutal murder by enforcement officer in front of public in USA.

George Floyd Can You Hear Me? The whole world is standing here for you!

It is full of injustice in our modern society, with my tiny brain I don't know why?

- Time to rethink! Time to reform!

Special Note To US President:

Mr. President, you might say that you are absolutely right in every aspect about this incident, but I have some personal views in this regard I like to share with you,

- George Floyd has 5 children and 2 grandchildren,

- Definitely after certain years, when time is up and matured, then they will find out the reason for killing his father and grandfather,

- Then what will happen, can you imagine that?

- **Who knows, there might be one (1) child would be similar like "Adolf Hitler",**

- Then what?

- You can imagine, Adolf Hitler killed 60 million Jewish people,

- Blame will go your advisory group and you too because during killing time (May-2020) you were the President of the United States of America (USA),

3: Jacob Blake Killing! August-2020

Jacob S. Blake is a 29-year-old African American man who was shot and seriously injured by police on August 23, 2020.

During an arrest, police officer Rusten Sheskey shot seven times at his back, with four shots hitting Blake.

The incident occurred in Kenosha, Wisconsin. During the encounter, Blake was tasered and scuffled with officers.

He was shot as he opened the driver's door to his SUV and leaned in. Three of Blake's sons were in the backseat.

The police shooting was followed by protests, which included rallies, marches, property damage, arson, and clashes with police.

Two protesters were also fatally shot in a confrontation with an armed civilian. Blake's name was invoked in protests in other cities as part of the "Black Lives Matter" movement, which has seen resurgence in the wake of high-profile killings by police officers in 2020.

This is pretty much brief description about Jacob Blake killing story in USA. I am not going for detail information but it is very clear how painful the story is!

Similarly, I am hopeless; I don't know what to say here.

- Where is justice?
- Where is my peace?

- I lost my language to talk!
- I am asking you where is solidarity in USA whereas **Republican** said in their Republican National Convention-2020 (RNC Day#1) that America is a "Land of Promised"!

It is an offensive, disgraceful and extreme racial conflict in the United States of America.

I am here to condemn!

The whole world is condemning against this racial brutal murder by enforcement officer in front of public in USA.

Jacob Blake Can You Hear Me? The whole world is standing here for you!
It is full of injustice in our modern society, with my tiny brain I don't know why?

- Time to rethink! Time to reform!

Special Note To US President:

Mr. President, you might say that you are absolutely right in every aspect about this incident, but I have some personal views in this regard I like to share with you.

- Jacob Blake has 3 children,

- Definitely after certain years, when time is up and matured, then they will find out the reason for killing his father,

- Then what will happen, can you imagine that?

- Who knows, there might be one (1) child would be similar like "Adolf Hitler",

- Then what?

- You can imagine, Adolf Hitler killed 60 million Jewish people,

- Blame will go your advisory group and you too because during killing time (August-2020) you were the President of the United States of America (USA),

4: Portland Killing! August-2020

(CNN)Police officials identified the man fatally shot Saturday night in downtown Portland, Oregon, amid clashes between pro-Trump groups and left-wing protesters as Aaron J. Danielson of Portland.

Police said **Danielson died** at the scene of a wound to the chest. He was positively identified by the Multnomah County Medical Examiner's Office, the Portland Police Bureau announced in a statement.

The far-right group Patriot Prayer, which has previously clashed with left-wing demonstrators, mourned Danielson's death.

The fatal shooting came after the "Trump 2020 Cruise Rally in Portland," in which supporters of President Donald Trump gathered in cars and drove in a caravan into Portland. Video footage from CNN affiliate KOIN showed pickups with American flags, "Thin Blue Line" flags, and Trump 2020 flags.

Portland police tried to keep the caravan out of downtown, but vehicles were able to "come into the downtown core," Police Chief Chuck Lovell said.

Police said there were instances of violence between demonstrators and counter-demonstrators when the caravan came through downtown.

Similarly again, I am hopeless; I don't know what to say here.

- Where is justice?
- Where is my peace?
- I lost my language to talk!
- I am asking you where is solidarity in USA whereas **Republican** said in their Republican National Convention-2020 (RNC Day#1) that America is a "Land of Promised"!

It is an offensive, disgraceful and extreme racial conflict in the United States of America.

I am here to condemn!

The whole world is condemning against this racial brutal murder by enforcement officer in front of public in USA.

It is full of injustice in our modern society, with my tiny brain I don't know why?

- Time to rethink! Time to reform!

5: Drive Through on Crowd in Portland! August-2020

Violent clashes were filmed in Portland when Trump supporters drove trucks into demonstrators and sprayed mace into the crowd. Source: Cory Elia,

Videos posted to social media show nasty clashes with Trump supporters using mace spray and paintball guns against opponents.

Multimedia Journalist Cory Elia shared a video on Twitter that shows several utes flying USA and Trump 2020 election flags driving through protesters and spraying them with what he described as "mace".

(CNN)A man drove his car into a group of protesters in downtown Portland, Oregon, injuring three, and then attempted to escape, a police statement says.

The incident, which happened early Wednesday, occurred as protesters marched in downtown Portland as part of the week's long protests calling for police reform.

It mirrors an incident last week in Henrico County, Virginia, where a man was arrested after he allegedly drove his car through a Black Lives Matter march.

Similarly again, I am hopeless; I don't know what to say here.

- Where is justice?

- Where is my peace?

- I lost my language to talk!

- I am asking you where is solidarity in USA whereas **Republican** said in their Republican National Convention-2020 (RNC Day#1) that America is a "Land of Promised"!

It is an offensive, disgraceful and extreme racial conflict in the United States of America.

I am here to condemn!

It is full of injustice in our modern society, with my tiny brain I don't know why?

- Time to rethink! Time to reform!

6: Israel & UAE Peace Agreement

On 13 August, **Israel** and the **UAE** signed an agreement mediated by U.S. President Donald Trump.

- Under the peace deal, **Israel** and the **UAE** will establish full diplomatic relations, with the **UAE** becoming the third Arab state, besides Egypt and Jordan, to fully **recognize Israel**,

- This is done by Donald Trump and his Son-in-law Jared Kushner,

Any peace deal, I would say it is a good job, it is a good idea. I appreciated for the peace deal as an ordinary man on this planet because I am always thinking positive.

Now it is a big question for this World?

- If the UAE and Israel can achieve peace deal, then why not **Israel-Palestine** can achieve peace deal?

- If the UAE and Israel can achieve peace deal, then why not **India-Kashmir-Pakistan** can achieve peace deal?

- If the UAE and Israel can achieve peace deal, then why not **Armenia-Azerbaijan** can achieve peace deal?

- If the UAE and Israel can achieve peace deal, then why not **Myanmar-Bangladesh** can achieve peace deal and so on around this world?

One of the fellow workers saying to me that in USA, they do not come in agreement between Democratic and Republican parties in many aspects, they always moving opposite direction, conflicts are there, issues are there, but they are busy and spending money to make a peace deal with third world countries,

How ridiculous it is!

I would say if their intention is really good for this world, then carry on peace deal!

Let the world know the future consequences in this regard,

What is happening in Kashmir, India & Pakistan?

The people are dying every day in Kashmir so called conflict territory in between India, Pakistan and China.

Same scenario happening here too, the whole world is silent for some unknown reasons.

United Nations (UN), G7, G8 and G20 country top leaders are unable to solve this problem, it is very hard to believe.

What does it mean?

What do you think about this matter?

This is another man-made critical case like Palestine and Israel issues.

What is the benefit end of the Day? People are killed every day, what kind of society we are living and holding?

It is full of injustice in our modern society, it is very hard to believe that G7, G8 and G20 country top leaders cannot solve this problems,

- Time to rethink! Time to reform! Time to change!

7: Israel & Palestine Conflicts

Each year how many peoples are killed in between Palestine and Israel conflict, it is unbelievable.

I am giving you year 2019 statistics.

- The Israeli government continued to enforce severe and discriminatory restrictions on Palestinians' human rights;
- Restrict the movement of people and goods into and out of the Gaza Strip;
- And facilitate the unlawful transfer of Israeli citizens to settlements in the occupied West Bank.

Between March 30 and November 19 of 2019,

- Security forces killed 189 Palestinian demonstrators,
- including 31 children and
- 3 medical workers,
- And wounded more than 5,800 with live fire.

Demonstrators threw rocks and "Molotov cocktails," used slingshots to hurl projectiles, and launched kites bearing incendiary materials, which caused significant property damage to nearby Israeli communities and in at least one instance, fired towards soldiers.

United Nations (UN), G7, G8 and G20 country top leaders are unable to solve this problem as of today.

It is very hard to believe!

What does it mean?

What do you think about this matter?

If you ask my honest opinion, I would say that I do not believe that they are unable to solve this issue.

There is lack of justice.

They all know what is happening and how to solve this crisis but they are not solving this issue rather,

- USA fueling Israel under the table, the whole world just watching as hopeless, helpless and they are unable to say something in this regard for unknown reasons, I do not know-why?
- United Nations (UN) is biased and seems they are blind, they can't see even though they have two (2) good eyes on their forehead, just doing eye-wash or brainwash of the world media,
- Europe and USA jointly silent in this regard,
- Muslim world silent and acting as coward and hypocrite,
- G7, G8, G20 country top leaders are biased too and seems they are blind too, not able to speak up in front of USA,

As a result, the final outcome is close to zero and if it is going on in this way, the outcome will remain zero. So I am hopeless, I don't know what to say here.

To be honest,

- G7, G8, G20 country top leaders,
- United Nations (UN),
- UN Veto Power Country Top leaders,

If the above body come forward based on neutral point of views, then this problem can be solved within very short period of time.

What is the benefit end of the Day?

People are killed every day, what kind of society we are living and holding?

It is full of injustice in our modern society, with my tiny brain but I don't know why?

Let the world think in this regard!

8: Who is Biggest Pollution Maker?

USA and China is a UN Veto Power Country,

Our expectations that they will maintain some standards so that the rest of the world can learn something from them,

But they are producing biggest world's air pollution in this world.

2ndly,

India also producing air pollution after USA and China,

India recently joins under UNSC as non-permanent member (as July-2020),

So the above all 3 countries are the permanent and non-permanent member of UNSC and they are producing biggest air pollution for this current world.

What do you think about this matter?

It is very hard to believe, Great countries!

<u>It is full of injustice, I don't know why & how they are still member of United Nations Security Council (UNSC)?</u>

<u>Let the world think about this matter!</u>

9: Ministry Allocation In Ontario

I am asking you a general question, who will be the Education Minister in a country like Canada, USA, UK?

Definitely, the answer would be the following but not limited and I believe most of you would be agree with me,

- The person should be well educated,
- Must have post-graduation,
- Have teaching or research experience in relation to education and industrial sector,
- It is better to have post-doctoral research experience (if someone have),
- Have publications in terms of journals, conference papers, workshops, seminars etc.,
- Have published books, modules etc.,
- Have huge experience worked as departmental head or dean of the faculty or vice-chancellor of the university,
- Have international work experience,
- I mean in depth knowledge on education and industry sector where h/she can suggest the academia,

- If the person holding the above criteria and become an education minister, nobody will ask and doubt about him/her,

Alternatively,
If you see our Ontario Education Minister,

https://en.wikipedia.org/wiki/Stephen_Lecce

From the above link, it is found that he has the following educational and work experience:

1. **Education**: Undergraduate in Political Science from University of Western Ontario,

2. **Work** Experience: <u>In fact, he does not have any work experiences as of 2020!</u>

3. **Political** Work Experience:
    - Lecce ran as a Progressive Conservative in the riding of King-Vaughan on June 7, 2018 and won.
    - On June 29, 2018, Lecce became the Parliamentary Assistant to Monte McNaughton, the Minister of Infrastructure.
    - On July 31, Lecce became Parliamentary Assistant to the Premier,

4. On June 20, 2019, he was sworn in as Ontario's Minister of Education,

5. Wonderful, Great Education Minister!

<u>It is a sort of injustice to Ontarians, with my tiny brain, I might be wrong. I don't know why & how he becomes an education minister in Ontario? Let the Canadian think about this matter!</u>

Dear Minister,

<u>Think for a minute the above criteria to become an education minister from the bottom of your heart not from the lip service of your mouth:</u>

- Minister, please don't misunderstand me, I respect you, but I am just criticizing the decision making systems to make our community a good one, nothing more than that.

- To me, it does not make any sense whereas many qualified people are working in this field in Ontario and h/she can become an education minister and serve the nation,

Therefore, I would say that your role as leader can bring the transparency into our modern community if you change your mind and accept positive criticism.

Stay connected based on strong moral path, we all together can build a healthy community by the grace of Almighty God.

10: Bill 21 In Ontario

In Canada, approximately 3.2% of the whole population is Muslims working as Canadians or permanent residents (PR) and it is considered as 2nd largest religion in Canada after Christianity.

Total approximately 1.0 million Muslims living all over in Canada.

The Quebec province has an estimated population of 8.2 million, which makes it the 2nd most populous province in Canada.

Out of 8.2 million populations, around 220,000 are Muslims living in Montreal, Quebec area.

The controversial Bill 21 became law in Quebec in June 2019 after being introduced in March.

This means that public workers in the province are **banned from wearing religious symbols** while on the job.

After a long debate, the bill went through with support from the Parti Québécois, thus formally banning teachers, police officers, judges and many other professionals from wearing items like hijabs, turbans, kippas, and crucifixes in the course of their duties.

What I understand from the above scenario listed below for your kind information:

- We are one more step away from the spiritual life,

- When society will be away from spiritual life, there will be disaster come down from God this is my understanding,

- You can see scenario during pandemic going on January-August 2020 on Germany, Italy, Spain, previously they banned religious symbols from their society even they banned the religious prayer, but during pandemic the authority permitted to resume the spiritual life again. What do we understand from those countries? Is it not enough that there is a God Who is controlling everything?

- I am requesting honorable Quebec premier through this chapbook that you may resume spiritual symbol while on the job,

- I have one recommendation about this matter to you, I might be wrong, but I am sharing my opinion, after allowing religious symbols while on job, if someone misuse it, abuse it, penalize them severely, punish them severely, think about this how to administer it and everybody would be happy,

- Canada is a multicultural country, so we have to think next 100 years in advance, not in autocratic way to pressurized people to follow it, then there might be dissatisfaction and one day it will burst,

- Another story I can share with you that I was in St Joseph Hospital, Hamilton for 3 days, I have noticed reception areas, private room, suite room all they have symbol of Crucifix pinned on the wall. It looks nice!

- But I was surprised and laughing, at the same time was shocked and remembering about Bill 21 in Quebec province,

<u>It is a sort of injustice! I don't know What caused, What happened & How it happened and it becomes a bill in Quebec? Time to rethink!</u>

11: Worldwide Muslim is a Terrorist-How?

Everyday around the world a lot of incidents, accidents, shooting, crimes are happening.

For example,
- In 46 weeks in 2019, there have been 45 school shootings in **USA**, By Elizabeth Wolfe and Christina Walker, **CNN**, Updated 4:13 AM ET, Tue November 19, 2019,

- **Los Angeles** (CNN) A teen whose birthday was Thursday went to his Southern California high school, pulled a pistol from his backpack and shot five classmates and himself in 16 seconds, authorities said. Two teens are dead after a 16-year-old gunman shot 5 classmates and himself in 16 seconds, cops say, By Jason Hanna, Cheri Mossburg and Steve Almasy, **CNN**, Updated 6:06 AM ET, Fri November 15, 2019,

- **Canada shooting:** Gunman kills at least 18 in Nova Scotia, A gunman disguised as a policeman killed at least 18 people, including a female Royal Canadian Mounted Police (RCMP) officer, in the worst mass shooting in Canada's modern history. The 12-hour rampage started late on Saturday and ended with a car chase. Police said the suspect shot people at different locations in Nova Scotia, many of them randomly. He was killed in a confrontation with police. He was reported to have been driving what looked like a police car. Canadian Prime Minister Justin Trudeau described the attack as "a tragedy".

There are many more examples I can add here but I will stop now. I can't imagine what's going on around this world and why? I am really hopeless.

I am asking you to read the articles and you will notice that most of the cases or incidents happened around the world is not by Muslims. Yes, some (very less compared to as a whole in this world) is done by Muslims.

But if one of the incident happen by Muslims, then print media will disseminate the news worldwide as it is a "Terrorist Attack" and it is done by "Muslims" and they are a "terrorist" whereas thousands of incidents are happening around the world every day by non-Muslims and print media are disseminating the news as "mentally ill or drug addicted or psychological problem stated by doctors or some other problem" but 100% confirm that they are not a terrorist.

- What a wonderful world we are living!
- Why do we blaming Muslims **only**, are they really terrorist?

So what do you think to the above statistics?

Think for a minute the above information from the bottom of your heart not from the lip service of your mouth.

Let the world think about this message!

With my tiny brain, it is full of injustice among us! I don't know how the G7, G8 & G20 country top leaders of the world thinking about this, I am just sharing my opinion through this chapbook? Time to rethink! Time to reform!

12: France Teacher Beheaded-How?

This incident happened in the month of October, 2020 in Paris, France while COVID-19 is still around us and we are not fully open our economy yet.

French Teacher Beheaded After Showing Muhammad Cartoons in Class

A French high school history teacher who showed his students caricatures of Islam's Prophet Muhammad was beheaded today, October 16, in the suburbs of Paris, authorities said. The suspected killer was shot and killed by police.

Dear World Readers,
Try to imagine, try to understand from the neutral point of view the following:

- Is it school teacher's job to show the students in the class during regular school activities "the caricatures of Islam's Prophet Muhammad"?

- I can't imagine about this incident because it is so sensitive issue because of religion, regardless what religion you are belongs to,

- As a school teacher, you are not allowed to discuss such an issues because it will make the environment **toxic**, **bitter** and **unpleasant**, he should not discuss this matter anyway, it is sort of unethical component to discuss in class,

However, there is another article from online news portal, I have noticed as follows:

Teacher in Paris suburb beheaded for discussing caricatures of Prophet Muhammad; Macron terms it 'Islamist terrorist attack'

French President **Emmanuel Macron** denounced what he called an "Islamist terrorist attack" and urged the nation to stand united against extremism. The teacher had discussed caricatures of Islam's Prophet Muhammad with his class, authorities said.

At this point, I would like to **criticize** French President **Emmanuel Macron**, saying that you made a great mistake saying "Islamic Terrorist Attack".

What I am trying to say in this regard as follows:

- You should **condemn** this brutal murder who did, no doubt, this is your first job as a President of the country,
- **Second**, you should declare that no school teacher is allowed to discuss such a religious sensitive issues during school activities going on now and in future, it is strictly prohibited and let him **penalize** for his mistakes as per education ministry rules and regulations and let the world know in this regard the real facts,
- **Third**, you should declare that no one is allowed to draw a caricature of Prophet of any religion, regardless because it is a religious sensitive issues among this **corrupted** world, it is strictly prohibited from now and on wards,

- **Fourth**, the person who killed a French high school history teacher, punish him **severely** as per local law and order so that the rest of the world can learn from this incident,
- **Fifth,** disclose the real facts with **evidence** in front of the public and let the rest of the world know in this regard,
- **Sixth,** this issue will be solved, nobody will argue in this regard, you will be **saluted** by the rest of the world, I guess,

But in contrary, you made a great mistake in my eyes:

- I would like to say that as a French President you have created a problem saying that "Islamic Terrorist Attack" without proper justification,
- The blame goes to your "political advisor", it is not a wise decision to speak in such a manner,
- You have **hurt** the people of the **second largest religion** in this world, you should **count** them,
- You have **hurt** the 25% of the current world's population, you should **count** them,
- I feel **shame** for you! Emmanuel Macron you have **degraded** yourself as a President of the United Nations Veto Power Country, FRANCE,

- You did not solve the problem rather you have created **man-made problem** in this current corrupted world, and you are responsible this problem,

Mr. Macron, look back the history of your country, how you treated people last 200 years, even now for African countries, you will see "autocratic, rude, dictatorship leadership attitude and behavior" in the past.

Yes, you did, you don't feel shy for the past history?

You should feel shy and regret!

Mr. Macron, my friend, read the history, you will be changed for sure, I am 100% guaranteed!

- You have **superpower** to shut down more than 70 Masjids in your country?
- You have **superpower** to draw a caricature of Islam's Prophet Muhammad in your country?
- You have **superpower** to burn religious holy book Al-Quran in your country?
- You have **superpower** to arrest 7% Muslims minority in your country?

Roughly seven (7%) Muslims are in your country; you are **pressing**, **insulting**, and **attacking** them, why?

Pressing, **insulting**, and **attacking** the minority people, IS IT FREEDOM OF SPEECH?

Who give you this authority?

Mr. Macron, try to understand FROM YOUR HEART NOT FROM YOUR LIP SERVICE, if other people draw a caricature of your own religious Prophet and fueling and advertising with the governmental support, then what will be your feelings?

Please think in such a manner, do not be a mad and do not make the world unrest.

We are on top of fire!

I saw your tweet on October 25, 2020 @1.36 PM; you wrote there "you will always be on the side of human dignity and universal values"

You are supporting your people to draw a caricature of other people's religion Islam's Prophet Muhammad (SWT) and displaying in a large building and so on.

At the same time, you are tweeting that you will always be on the side of human dignity and universal values.

What does it mean?

You are creating a "**Double Standard**"!

You have degraded yourself "**Macron**"!

Fantastic! I was laughing to see your tweet!

What a wonderful **corrupted** world we are living!

Why do we blaming Muslims **only**, are they really terrorist?

So what do you think to the above brutal murder?

Think for a minute the above information from the bottom of your heart not from the lip service of your mouth as President of United Nations Veto Power Country FRANCE,

Let the world think about this message!

It is full of injustice among us!

13: G7, G8 and G20 Country Top Leaders

1. G8 & G20 country top leaders blaming each other country and trying to show up their **superpower** or pretending like having everyone has superpower or **nuclear power**, indirectly, they are threatening each other,

2. G8 & G20 country top leaders are not trusting each other country and most of the time they goes by,

    - on "skeptical mode",
    - then "on hold",
    - then "on pause",
    - then after high level communication back and forth among them,
    - then "on running mode",
    - then it goes "trustless".
    - The rest of the world becomes victims!
    - What I am trying to say that we have to trust each other and we must have "positive trust attitude mechanism" so that we can feel confident each other.

    For example,

    - ❖ Vladimir Putin claims Russia has developed first COVID vaccine (August-2020) which is ready for usage and it is safe and it has long time immunity,

- ❖ Whitehouse experts were **highly** skeptical on the first news, not only that US official accuses Russia of hacking research,
- ❖ Then Russia dismisses that,
- ❖ Vladimir Putin also claims that one of his daughter has taken it as test basis, she is good in health now,
- ❖ Still skeptical fight started on this issue among them,
- ❖ Wonderful!
- ❖ Carry on "UN Veto Power Country"!
- ❖ I am proud of you!

So as an ordinary general people of this planet I am asking you where to go? Who do I trust in this planet?

Whereas UN Veto Power Country (Russia) claims something positive for humanity and other Veto Power Country (USA) rejects on first news and goes on skeptical mode, it means that we are on top of fire.

Very Dangerous Symptoms!!

It is alike as pandemic is on the way,

So time to rethink, time to reform the systems,

3. G8 & G20 country top leaders threatening by nuclear test each other country and trying to control each other,

    - but I am trying to say that this is not the way to control this world,

    - We have to change this control policy, time to rethink, time to reform the systems,

4. G7, G8 & G20 country top leaders imposing sanctions on the poor countries without justification and United Nations (UN) did not do any actions in this regard, it seems that UN works as if like puppets,

5. G7, G8, G20 and most of the country top leaders, top 250 billionaire and other respective high level officials **stealing** assets by a pen, it becomes fashion use a pen and steal the property,

6. G7, G8, G20 and most of the country top leaders, top 250 billionaire and other respective high level officials **lying** and it becomes a fashion to lie in our modern society,

7. G7, G8 & G20 country top leaders common attributes are given below with other countries:

For example,

United States of America (USA):

- If USA likes you, there would be very good relationship with you, they will **kiss** you, no doubt,
- If USA likes you, then you will be on top of their head and you can **dance** over there, no problem,
- It is 100% legal and valid worldwide, legitimate and tested,

Oppositely,

- If they don't like you, there would be very **bitter** relationship with you,
- If they don't like you, then you will be under their **foot**,
- You will be kicked out from every aspects in this world,
- What kind of attitude and principle they are holding!

- I am hopeless!
- I am senseless!

- They are UN Veto Power Country Top Leaders!
- Carry on "UN Veto Power Country"!

Russia:

- I heard from one of my friend that if you criticize the president of the country of Russia, the next day you might be disappeared or will be fined or will be arrested,
- What kind of administration is there!

- United Nations (UN) is totally silent or blind in this regard!
- United Nations (UN) works as "deaf and dumb" in this regard!

- I am hopeless!
- I am senseless!

- They are UN Veto Power Country Top Leaders!

- Carry on "UN Veto Power Country"!

China:

- It seems as if innocent country in the world to me!
- During conference meeting or conversation, they smile, and the value of their smile is invaluable, you are not able to purchase this smile, they have God gifted smile,
- They have high level of patience and tolerance, they can pretend as if they understand nothing,
- They have very good relationship all over the world,
- They make happy every country in this world and they want to make you happy as you wish,
- Their supply chain is very outstanding, like they have very expensive product to supply, they have very cheap product if you want, they have free product as well, now everything depends on you,
- What a wonderful country it is!
- It is only 1 country in this universe! Called CHINA!
- I am hopeless too!

- They are UN Veto Power Country Top Leaders!
- Carry on "UN Veto Power Country"!

North Korea:

- North Korea has not very good diplomatic relationship with the rest of the world, they do not care any country in this world, and it is big question, why?

- The United Nations (UN) is unable to do some legal actions against North Korea; why-it is a big question for UN?
- United Nations (UN) works as "deaf and dumb" in this regard!

- UN Veto Power Country why they are silent in this regard? They are unable to do any legal action too,

- I heard from one of my friend that if you criticize the president of the country, the next day you will be killed or disappeared,

- What kind of administration is there!

- I am hopeless!

Canada:

- It is a only natural tolerance based country in the world,
- They accept you while other country rejects you,

  For examples,
  - ➢ USA rejects refugees and Canada welcomes them!

  - ➢ USA rejects immigration temporarily and Canada accepts and welcomes them!

  - ➢ USA stops funding for WHO and Canada supports them!

- What a wonderful **match**!

- I am not sure how the foreign affairs advisory groups working on it between these two (2) countries,

- To me, it is very hard to maintain from one side whereas other side does not cooperate, the ultimate outcome goes negative!

UAE:

- One of the rich country in gulf region,
- Recently they sent COVID-19 medical aids to Palestine,
- Palestinian Authority rejects COVID-19 aid flown from UAE to Israel

For example,

> - The Palestinian government said it was not coordinated with them regarding the medical supplies.
> - Can you imagine UAE sent reliefs to Palestine and they do not have any official communication in between 2 countries,
> - UAE flight landed in Israel not in Palestine, citing "sovereignty" concerns,
> - I can't imagine how it is possible in this 21st century!

- What a wonderful relation between them!
- I am not sure how the foreign affairs advisory council working on it between these 2 countries,

With my tiny brain, it is a sort of injustice around the globe, Time to rethink! I am hopeless!

14: Spiritual Worlds

We are not following the pretty basic 10-15 commandments or guidelines as per Holy Scripture given by God to religious Prophet for those who believe in oneness of God. Yes some of them are following but their numbers are very low.

For example, every religion said,

- Do not **lie**, but in real life we are lying, it is a fashion for our modern society to tell a lie!

- Do not **steal**, but in real life, whenever we have chance, we are stealing by **a pen**, we are not following whatsoever,

- Do not do **adultery**, but in real life, whenever we have chance, we are doing adultery,

- Do respect or **honor** parents, but in real life, we are not respecting our parents, during their old age, we sent them retire home care Centre, even we do not have time to visit them weekly basis,

There are many more examples, I can add here but I will stop now, think for a minute, why we are not following what God said to us. What's wrong with that!

It is full of injustice in our modern society,

- Time to rethink! Time to reform!

15: Technological Advancement Worlds

We are living in 21st century and enjoying science based technology in our daily life. I recalled my childhood, teacher asked me, "Science is blessing or curse" I replied it is a blessing, teacher gave me a smile. But nowadays in 21st century, it is a sort of curse. WHY?

We all should know this story; due to technological advancement we are facing troubles in our modern society:

Fraud, Scamming-there are many kinds of fraud,

- Credit card, Master card, Visa card, debit card all types card under fraud, it is a kind of technological threats,
- Where is the control to stop these threats?
- Control KEY with whom?
- Who is controlling these threats?
- In this 21st century it is out of control because hackers are so active where general people cannot cope with them,

For example,

I am giving one real life example, one of my close relative, h/she was a student at the university level, doing summer job in Ontario and earned around $8000 and planning to do something towards his/her fall intake. Before start his fall intake, his bank account was attacked by a scammer and h/she lost almost full amount what h/she earned during summer job.

I have chance to talk with them, then I heard, they went to bank and discussed the matter what happened and the bank personnel explained to them that it is happening every day and it is out of our control, we are not able to refund the money what you lost from your bank account.

Then they went to local police station, filled a case and all information is noted. Police said, they will investigate on it and let you know the outcome. After 6 weeks later, they got a letter from police department that says that we are unable to find the scammer even though scammer has cell phone contact and email address.

The technological failure part is that scammer communicated using cell phone and email id, our police department failed to investigate this cell phone number registered belongs to whom?

When I bought a SIM in Ontario from Bell or Rogers or any other service providers, my all address and contact details are filled out and recorded. Then why Ontario police department failed to get information from a scammer phone contact, I don't understand why and how it is not possible?

I am not against technological advancement, I like it, I love it and every day I am enjoying it, but my concern:
- Where is the control?
- Who can control it?

My personal opinion technological expert should have control on it; otherwise it is big threat for our modern society.
- One day this threat will kill all of us,

- One day this threat will damage all of us,
- This is the time today we must think about this; otherwise it will be late to rethink!

2nd,

- Competition of nuclear testing worldwide, nobody cares about this threat,
- Biological warfare, e.g. COVID-19, currently we are suffering for this threat,
- I believe "Young generation" end of next 10 years will not talk anymore, they will communicate through text message, voice mail, twitter, instagram, facebbok, and so on, and I am doubtful, they might go on silent mode, then we will lost our young generation,

So I am requesting G7, G8 & G20 country top leaders including top 50 rich people in this world come forward and save this world, otherwise due to technological advancement, one day this technological threat will kill us.

I am not against technological advancement, my concern there should be a KEY so that our enforcement department can detect the criminals and control the crimes happening around the world that is my big concern, nothing more than that.

There are many more examples, I can add here about technological advancement but I will stop now, think for a minute.

It is full of injustice in our modern society, with my tiny brain but I don't know WHY? Time to rethink! Time to reform!

16: Bill Gates Outstanding Speech

This is my personal views that I could not find any significant progress towards what he discussed based on his TEDTALK given in 2015 and also discussed the matter with US President in 2016.

To me it is a sort of **polite cheating** towards 7 billion people in this world. This is my views towards him, I might be wrong based on global perspectives, but I found doing business for his own foundation.

The details are listed below for your information:

In 2015 there is a TEDTALK given by Bill Gates (links given below), "The next outbreak? We are not ready"!!!

https://www.youtube.com/watch?v=6Af6b_wyiwI
The next outbreak? We're not ready | Bill Gates

Bill Gates talked to us as if he knows everything what coming next! Let's look into the following transcripts from his lecture:

1. If anything kills over 10 million peoples in the next few decades, it's most likely to be a highly infectious virus rather than a war.
2. Not missiles, but microbes.
3. Now, part of the reason for this is that we have invested a huge amount in nuclear deterrents.
4. But we have actually invested very little in a system to stop an epidemic.
5. We are not ready for the next epidemic.

He mentioned some key pieces are listed below:

- We need strong health systems in poor countries that where mother can give birth safely; kids can get all their vaccines.
- We need medical reserve corps
- We need pair medical and military
- We need to do simulations, germ games, not the war games, so that we can see where the holes are.

Look at the end of the talk; he **politely** said we need lots of advanced R&D in areas of vaccines and diagnostics. There are some big breakthroughs, like the Adeno-associated virus, that could work very, very quickly.

Now I don't have an exact budget for what this would cost, but I am quite sure it is very modest compared to the potential harm. The World Bank estimates that if we have a worldwide flu epidemic, global wealth will go down by **over three (3) trillion dollars**, and we would have millions and millions of deaths.

This investment offers significant benefits beyond just being ready for the epidemic. The primary healthcare, the R&D, those things would reduce global health equity and make the world more just as well as more safe. So I think this should absolutely be a priority.

There is no need to panic!!!!!! We don't have to hoard cans of spaghetti or go down into the basement. But we need to get going, because time is not on our side. In fact, there is one positive thing that can come out of the Ebola epidemic; it is that it can serve as an early warning, a wake-up call, to get ready.

If we start now, we can be ready for the next epidemic. Thank you.

- All his ideas are materialistic i.e. excessively concerned with material possessions, I mean money-oriented.

- He knows as if COVID-19 is on the way to attack this world, how, it is a question mark?

- Bill Gates said in an interview with STAT two years ago that he had urged President Trump to invest in technologies to respond to a pandemic.

- "The president was kind enough to spend time with me, and one of the issues I brought up is this opportunity to build new tools that would help us deal with a pandemic,'' said Gates, who has long warned of the possibility of a global disease outbreak.

- He added: "It is strange that this risk, that the world isn't doing more. We talk about doing more when we have smaller epidemics like Ebola and Zika, but then the actual follow-up is pretty modest. We think the idea of spending what would be a tiny part of the budget to be ready for a pandemic makes sense.''

Dear Readers,
What do we understand from the above conversation with President Donald Trump in 2016 with BG, it is very hard to comprehend, to me it seems BG knows present and future of what is happening in this world, in a nutshell, BG knows as if someone told him before. He is really outstanding man in this world.

Bill Gates (BG) can reach the whole world within 24 hours, he has that kind of capability, he can deliver the good or bad message to this world within short time and I believe people will listen to him.

But personally I felt very upset after listening his outstanding lecture on future pandemic because it is money-making future dream, because he is asking the world to gather **3 trillion** dollars to do research on vaccines to protect future pandemic under his own foundation, it is totally followed by materialistic life for his own business.

He never asks in his speech to 7 billion people in this world to the following questions:
- To be a good human based on morality,
- Build a good work ethics,
- Build a good ethics in family oriented life, (no divorce, no break up, live in harmony etc.,)
- Build a good ethics in neighborhood oriented,
- Finally become a good human to support a community or society, a family, as a result, you are supporting the whole world,
- He is asking for dollars only!

17: Own House/Family

1. The chemistry between husband and wife are not satisfactory level in most of the family, always conflict is there, as a result **divorce rate** is going high in western countries,

2. No proper bonding among family members, as a result, no respect among spouses, parents, children each other, this is the time to think about this, this is in crucial stage in western countries,

3. Some parents did not give priority to their children when their children were small and young and needed help from their parents. Parents go away and they prefer their likings. What kind of bonding or relationship between parents and children are there, it is a million dollar question?

4. Today's parent does not follow about parenting style like "Brick-wall parents or Back-bone parents or Jellyfish parents",

5. Some family members yes of course they are good and positive minded but their numbers are very limited,

It is a sort of injustice in our modern society; let the western culture think about this matter! We have to come up with solution; otherwise big misfortune is waiting for all of us! Our G7, G8, and G20 country top leaders no time to think about this, what causes this injustice!

18: Local Community/Neighborhood

1. We don't know our neighborhood from the heart, we just know by face; even sometimes we don't have their contact information. In case of emergency, we are unable to contact, unable to help,

2. We don't know our roommate very well if you live in a rental house from the heart, we just know by face; even **sometimes** we don't have their contact information. In case of emergency, we are unable to contact, unable to help.

    - In case, there is conflict for some reason, then they do not come forward for further discussion and solve the problem rather treating roommates as hypocrites, bad people, go away etc…,
    - This is very crucial stage in western societies,

3. We hate each other, sometimes we don't want to see their face each other, this is a real fact,

4. Some community people drug addicted, mentally ill because of the existing systems,

5. During gathering or party time, in our own community programs, people are talking continuously about Facebook, twitter, instagram, local and world politics, personal business. We don't care whether we are lying or faking, does not

matter, the main agenda, I have to say something in front of this gathering, but whenever you start spiritual talk, most of them gently left the place,

6. Everybody showing some sort of pride regardless what we are!

   For examples,

   - Rich people always pressing low income people anyway,
   - Rich neighborhood always showing up egotistic behavior to low income neighborhood,

7. Some Neighborhood yes of course they are good and positive minded but their numbers are very limited,

It is a sort of injustice in our modern society,

- Let the western culture think about this matter!

- We have to come up with solution; otherwise big misfortune is waiting for all of us!

19: Workplace

1. Some white skin supervisors think that they are master of everything and super smart, it seems they know everything, treat workers, co-workers differently, which is not acceptable way to treat people in workplace,

2. Some supervisors threatening the workers, co-workers (hidden **discrimination** is always there!),

3. Some white skin guy or supervisors twisted the scenario and make the situation worse, as a result creating a problem, not solving a problem, this is another problem in the work place, then go to union, talk to them and it is a long process to solve the overall situation, in the meantime, both parties suffer a lot,

4. Some supervisors fired the workers, co-workers during probation period without real cause or justification, sort of **white supremacy** is there in silent manner, nobody knows but it is there!

5. During gathering in workplace, some supervisors are giving talk, for example, it takes only 5 minutes to wrap up, but h/she is talking continuously, wasting time,

6. Some supervisors educational background "under qualified", even they do not have College or Bachelor degree, grade 12 maximum, but they are supervising all types of people in the plant. I am not sure what type of miracle h/she has in this

regard, they are treating people with differently with hidden discrimination, as a result, the environment become toxic and bitter.

- Respective authority should look after this issue especially in western countries,

7. Some supervisors yes of course they are good and positive minded, they have vision for life-long learning, caring other fellow workers but their numbers are very limited,

It is a sort of injustice in our modern society,

- Let the western culture think about this matter!
- We have to come up with solution; otherwise bitter and toxic environment would be around workplace which is not good for all of us!

One Practical Real Life Example:

Scenario#1:

Let's say you as black or brown color worker or Asian working with white people or with many other people. You notice that white skin guy did a big mistake and he is repeating this mistake and h/she somehow hide it continuously, nobody knows except you.

One day you inform your supervisor not officially, just off record, just giving him some head's up about his work habits.

The guy knows from his supervisor that I have informed him about his work habits,

You are in big trap now.

Scenario#2:

Some other day, suddenly he is asking, hey did you do that piece of work, if you reply, no or not yet.

Then he will say wow, you did not doing your work properly, even though your mistake is very small compared to his mistakes,

He intentionally nailed you because he knows that you have told something against him to his Supervisor.

Scenario#3:

Blaming game started now,

He is making story now,

He is twisting the real story now,

For examples,

Let's say his mistakes weight is 50kg,

&

Your mistake weight is hardly 1 kg,

Now the white guy with some other white skin discussing the matter and make a great **twist** story against you.

Now you are on big trap because management people most of them are white skin, they are always inclined to them.

Finally, you are in such a situation that you have to surrender them or apologize them or they will go for action against you.

Your 1 kg weight of mistakes, they will twist or create it like weight is more than 50kg.

The management will believe them because the way they will twist or create the story, the way they twist the story, as it is real story, it is like a cinematic drama.

Problems Can Be Solved Within One (1) Minute But It Takes Long Time

Today in our modern society, we are facing a lot of social problems. These problems can be solved within short period of time if everybody accepts **criticism positively**.

When you start practice criticizing yourself and accept criticism positively from outsiders, then half of the modern society problems will be solve automatically, if you don't believe me, then try out yourself first time, it will be self-proven automatically.

Social scientists, UN, G7, G8, G20 country top leaders, top 50 richest people, and spiritual leaders have significant impact to solve this problem; all should come forward to help our modern society.

Print media like TVs, newspapers must broadcasting and publishing about "human morality development" "ethical knowledge" program for mass people for this current **corrupted** world "how to reduce social problems" from our modern society!

If this earth starts **vomiting** i.e. before the earth discharges its burdens [99:2], then it will be too late to go back to normal stage, it means we are done!

It is a trillion dollar question for this modern society how to solve a problem within short period of time!

Summary From All Above Systemic Injustice Scenario

- It is found that **systemic injustice is available everywhere, every sector, every corner in our modern society or community and all over the world**.

- To me based on my personal views, current world is not functioning properly due to the following causes:

  - UN Veto Power country specially USA, China, France and Russia not working the way they supposed to work, they are **vindictive** in nature,
  - G7, G8 and G20 country top leaders are not acting positively, they are **vindictive** in nature too,
  - Top 50 richest people in this world their mind are just business oriented, if they wish they can change this world, they have a lot of room to change this **corrupted** world, but they are crazy for their own business,
  - Religious leaders are not acting properly, they are seems coward and confined,
  - Teenagers, adults, leaders, and non-believers nobody is working properly, then how do you expect a healthy community in this 21st century?

- So at a glance, the following activities changes rapidly negatively, it is an alarming rate, please have a look,

  - Crime rate goes high,
  - Murder rate goes high,
  - Divorce rate goes high,
  - Drinking alcohol rate goes high,
  - Vaping e-cigarette rate goes high,
  - Gambling rate goes high,
  - Gun man rate goes high,
  - LGBT rate goes high,
  - Environmental pollution making rate goes high,
  - Death in custody rate goes high,
  - Hate rate goes high,
  - The widespread & systemic torture of persons in custody by police, security forces and prison guards goes high,

So we are on top of fire, believe me!!!

- Therefore, God become upset due to all kinds of injustice and then what will happen?

- The ultimate result goes as natural calamities like Epidemic, Pandemic, and COVID-19, which we cannot see with our naked eyes, but they are killing us, we are unable to invent the vaccine within short period of time using science and technology we have so far,

- Can you imagine that our teenagers, adults, leaders, religious leaders, non-believers all are somehow, somewhere corrupted or brainwashed, then how do you expect a healthy community will be exist in this 21st century?

- My personal views, you cannot control this community in this traditional way, you must think differently, you must change the control policy.

- As an ordinary general person, we can't do anything; it should come from G7, G8 and G20 country top leaders including top 50 richest people in this world,

- Did you ask yourself or did we ask ourselves that why the above systemic injustice happening around worldwide? How to get rid of from those injustices?

- The only reason I would say that God has given us some guidelines as per various holy scriptures explained the following in brief:

  ➢ how to live in this world,
  ➢ how to behave with others,
  ➢ what to eat,
  ➢ what not to eat,
  ➢ What to do and what not to do,

  ➢ But we are not following or caring at all, so God become very upset.

Then how do you expect a healthy community in this 21st century?

Dear G7, G8 & G20 Country Top Leaders

<u>Think for a minute the above all different scenario based on different circumstances from the bottom of your heart not from the lip service of your mouth:</u>

Please don't misunderstand me.

I have criticized the whole world including myself, my family members, my community members, teenagers, adults, leaders, non-believers, religious leaders, top 50 richest people, and you as G7, G8, G20 country top leaders.

My intention not to hurt any individual like you,

I solely criticize the systems and decision making mechanism, which run this society so that it can be improved and as a result we all will enjoy the better healthy life in this world instead of creating or making disaster like an epidemic or pandemic.

I am just criticizing the systems to make our community a good one, nothing more than that.

If someone is hurt after reading my chapbook, please forgive me, again this is not my intention to hurt you at individual level.

I believe in <u>positive criticism</u> on everything in this universe and this can improve the systems.

In this chapbook, I have positively, constructively, practically, logically and partially criticized about China, USA, France, Russia and Canada for improvements based on my judgment so that we can stay in racism free society with all types of people in multicultural environment.

Our society is a full of injustice, full of fool, no doubt. It is in very crucial stage now.

Therefore, I would say that your role as leader, as richest person have significant tremendous impact which can bring the "transparency" into our modern society if you change your policy and accept positive criticism.

So what is next?

At this time, I will discuss briefly about duty of "advisory group" of US President and advisors of G7, G8, G20 leaders.

Let's see next Chapter 3 for more specific information!!

CHAPTER 3

Advice To US President & His Advisory Groups

In this chapter, I will discuss briefly about "advisory group" of US President as well as G7, G8, G20 leader's advisory group activities. I believe the role of advisory group has tremendous effects of Presidents decision, what to say and what not to say, what to do and what not to do and finally stay in peaceful positive reliable safe position.

I might be wrong based on your perspectives or global perspectives or might be correct, decision is yours, but I am just sharing my views.

Before telling my ideas, I would like to share with you that I do not like to explain the facts in zigzag way; usually I focus to the main point directly to solve the problem rather working in the periphery of a circle. That is my style, just sort of heads-up for my readers.

My focus not care who will win in this upcoming US Election-2020, I am focusing based on morality, based on principles for a healthy community in this world.

Please have a look!

1: Advice goes to Mr. US President

It is my honor, I feel proud that I am going to write-up something about you. If my views goes against you, do not take it by heart, please forgive me, this is not my intention to hurt you, just criticizing the "decision making mechanism" of your governing system, nothing more than that.

You might say that you are absolutely right in every aspect during your regime (2016-2020), I have nothing to argue with you, but I have some personal views about your tenure and also 2nd term candidacy from Republican Party for 2020-election.

- If you read the first few incidents written in "Chapter 2 Injustice Happening Around The World/Globe" from your bottom of the heart, then you will notice that it is not an usual circumstances, some sort of abnormal, systemic injustice towards your nation,

- It is an offensive, disgraceful and extreme racial conflict in the history of United States of America as per my tiny knowledge,

- Again, you might say that you are 100% correct, I am not arguing with you.

- You can imagine the story of Adolf Hitler who killed 60 million Jewish people because of simple matter happened in his school life what we know from the history,

But I am **afraid** that you might create from your black community another "boy" like "**Adolf Hitler**". You know the story of Adolf Hitler who has killed 60 million Jewish people during that time just for **little** discrimination in his school life by his teacher.

- All blames will go to you and your advisory group because during your tenure and 2020-election campaign, few Americans were killed and you were the President of the United States,

What I am trying to say that as a World Leader, do always best thing for mankind, people will remember you, do not follow "autocratic leaders attitude" in the history of World.

- Just imagine momentarily, end of your 2nd term, you will be no longer in position, but people will remember you as an "autocratic-dictator-racist President" in the world history,

- You will be criticized by the rest of the world,

- What will you gain from this regime?

- Absolutely NOTHING!!

I know you did some great accomplishments and some contradictory facts too based on my own perspectives during your tenure, but do not forget, you are not the only one.

Let the "young generation" to come in under Republican Party and let them "take over" the whole responsibility and you go back to advisory group and advise them what to do and what not to do as a good man. People will remember you; God will bless you if you do good things for mankind.

Mr. President,

- New York City does not welcome you to visit the city,
- Similarly, Kenosha City does not welcome you to visit the city,
- There are many more incidents to write-up here, but I will stop now,
- So it is not enough to resign from the Government?
- I would say "Enough is enough"!!

2: Advice goes to Advisory Group

It is my honor, I feel proud that I am going to share something with "**advisory group of US President**". Again if my view goes against you, do not take it by heart, please forgive me.

This is not my intention to hurt you, just criticizing you because you have given the "decision making advice" to US President,

- It is not a joke, to advise US President as an "Advisor", it is really a very hard job, very tough job,

- It is not a joke, it is really a very responsible and accountable job for those who will be assigned,

You might say that you are absolutely right in every aspect during your work period, I have nothing to argue with you, but I have some personal views about your advice philosophy and consequences and let the world know in this regard.

- I know all of you are in expert level working as an advisor of US President,
- I know you can give talk with speed level **200km/hour nicely, gently, and convince** the people,
- It looks good even though you are doing a polite cheating, I am not sure how to explain here, but I am trying to explain,

My apology, I am not an expert in analyzing USA election, but I have general feeling as an ordinary man on this planet based on present abnormal circumstances happening around the globe and that's why I am going to write-up here for you.

Let's have a look from your heart.

- If you read "What USA Election-2020 Brought Back to Us!" written in "Chapter 1" from your bottom of the heart, then you will notice that it is not acceptable anyway because USA is one of the permanent member of United Nations Veto Power Country, USA has high level weight and dignity, people respect USA as leading nation and will respect if it is maintained,

- Another reason currently USA leading the whole world and your position as an adviser to US President has tremendous impact about his success or failure in upcoming election and also worked as future world leader,

- Another reason currently USA holding the position as a major "donor country" and your position as an adviser to US President has tremendous impact about foreign country relationship and get support from them,

- You are the main ingredient in "decision making systems" because your every single input, every single words shakes US President's position what to do or what to say or what not to do etc.,

- I mean you are one of the "Key Personnel" in US President's life during his regime,

- Can you imagine "Who Are You"?

- Did you recognize "You" as an advisor to US President?

- You are like a "**Big Catalyst**",

- You can change or damage or you can build your own country and also the rest of the world,

- Can you imagine "Who Are You"?

- You are an advisor of US President of the United States, **WOW**!

Based on my tiny observance, monitoring and evaluating during pre-election stage campaign, I found USA Election-2020 brought back to us as follows:

- USA Election-2020 campaign brought back to us a lot of things listed below but not limited to,

  - attacking,
  - blaming,
  - insulting,
  - back biting,
  - pressing,
  - pounding,
  - hammering,
  - forcing,
  - hating,
  - lying,
  - polite cheating,
  - polite religious cheating,
  - priding and so on,

It is an offensive, disgraceful and extreme racial campaign in the history of United States of America as per my tiny knowledge,

Not only that, during first Presidential debate on September 29, 2020 moderator Chris Wallace of Fox News said "A terrible missed opportunity": Chris Wallace laments losing control of the presidential debate, to control and handle both of President Donald Trump and President Nominee under Democratic Party Joe Biden, what do you think about his comments?

I saw some election campaign in South Asia,

For examples, India, Bangladesh & Pakistan,

- I thought their election campaign was very bad, and dirty,
- But as of today (September-October, 2020), I am comparing their election campaign with USA Election-2020 campaign, found pretty much same and similar,

What does it mean?

It means in South Asia, they do not care what other people said to them, most of the time they applied "might is right or tit-for-tat" principle during their election campaign, their main goal how to win in the election.

- They are super greedy for governmental power,
- They are super hungry for governmental power,
- So they do not follow real democracy,

Similarly, in USA election-2020, I saw same principle you as an advisor applied, it seems you do not care what the rest of the world will tell you,

- You applied "might is right or tit-for-tat" principle during your pre-election campaign time,
- It is similar pattern with in South Asia that main goal how to win in the election.

Few Questions Mr. Advisor

- ❖ Did you ever give advice to US President that Mr. President your campaign style is not appropriate, it is not acceptable way to reach voter's mind, people will condemn you at later stage,

- ❖ My question is very straight forward, did you ask Mr. US President the above question or not?

- ❖ It seems to me that you did not give proper advise to US President,

- ❖ It seems to me that you did not ask Mr. US President the questions,

- ❖
- ❖ Then my next question why not? What did you do?

- ❖ It is a Trillion Dollar Questions?

For examples,

- Portland campaign conflicts and 1 man died,

- Drive through on crowd and tit-for-tat attitude,

- Killing Jacob Blake with 7 shoots by police officer in day light period in front of a public,

- George Floyd killing and so on,

- Twitter removes information about COVID-19,

- The above activities are strongly unethical, against morality, and so on,

My question to you and I hope you will clear this message for the world readers!

If you did not give him such an advice, then blame will goes to you because you are considered as "key personnel" of US President as an advisor.

- Blame will goes to you because you are responsible for advice to the US President,

- It means you are failed to motivate to US President,

- It means you are not performed your job/duty as assigned to US President,

- It means you have taken advantage from Mr. President and your attention diverted somewhere for unknown reason, I might be wrong or might be correct, let the world reader to think in this regard,

- It means you are sold out somewhere based on my tiny knowledge, I might be wrong or might be correct, let the world reader to comment in this regard,

For examples,

Steve Bennon is charged with fraud in we build the wall campaign, he is under custody now,

So think for a minute about your role!

We are on top of fire!

What I am trying to say that as an "Adviser", do always best thing for mankind, do not follow "autocratic leadership attitude", then you will be blamed by the rest of the world.

- You will be criticized by the rest of the world,
- What will you gain from this job?
- Absolutely NOTHING!!

Let the "world readers" think about your role and activities in connection with US President from the neutral point of view as an Advisor to US President.

3: Advice goes to Mr. Pastor

It is my honor, I feel proud that I am going to write-up something about you Mr. Pastor. If my view goes against you, do not take it by heart, please forgive me.

This is not my intention to hurt you, just criticizing to you as you are a Pastor or Spiritual advisor of US President because you have given the "spiritual counsel" to US President.

You might say that you are absolutely right in every aspect what you advise to US President, I have nothing to argue with you, but I have some personal views about your spiritual counsel and let the world know in this regard.

- If you read the "What USA Election-2020 Brought Back to Us!" written in "Chapter 1" from your bottom of the heart, then you will notice that it is not anyway acceptable as per holy scriptures of "Bible" regardless of any religion,

- USA Election-2020 campaign brought back to us a lot of things listed below but not limited to,

    - attacking,
    - blaming,
    - insulting,
    - back biting,
    - pressing,
    - pounding,
    - hammering,
    - forcing,

- ➢ hating,
- ➢ lying,
- ➢ cheating,
- ➢ priding and so on,

It is an offensive, disgraceful and extreme racial campaign in the history of United States of America as per my tiny knowledge,

Few Questions Mr. Pastor

- ❖ Did you ever tell to US President that Mr. President I prayed to Jesus Christ (God) for you, for your success in front of all,

- ❖ But as per Bible, the above campaign attributes what you are applying, you are not allowed to do that during your 2020-election campaign,

- ❖ It is strongly prohibited in the Bible.

- ❖ This is the question to you and I hope you will clear this message for the world readers!

If you did not give him such an advice, then blame will goes to you because you are considered as "spiritual advisor" of US President.

- Blame will goes to you because you are responsible for spiritual counsel to the US President,

- It means you are failed to motivate spiritually to US President,

- It means you are sold out somewhere based on my tiny knowledge, I might be wrong or might be correct, let the world reader to comment in this regard,

So think for a minute about your role!

We are on top of fire!

There might a question mark how a spiritual leader is sold out?

For examples,

In 2015, according to the public Form 990 Tax Return in USA, **Ravi Zacharias** and his wife reported earning a combined total of USD $523,926 from his non-profit Ravi Zacharias International Ministries (RZIM).

He said it is not-profit Ministries.

What I am trying to say that as a Spiritual Leader, do always best thing for mankind, do not follow "autocratic leadership attitude", then **first** you will be blamed by rest of the world and then secondly and **permanently** you will be blamed by God Who is watching you in every moment,

- Just imagine momentarily,
- Every day you are touching the holy scriptures "BIBLE" and if you are doing religious polite cheating with your Bible and also with public, then what will happen,
- Then after some time, you will be no longer in that position, you have to die as you believe in one God,
- So what will happen in the Day of Judgment?
- Think for a minute in this regard,

- What will you gain from this journey/money?

- Absolutely it is FIRE, NOTHING MORE THAN THAT!! NOTHING ELSE!!

Let the "world readers" think about your role and activities in connection with US President from the neutral point of view as Pastor or spiritual advisor to US President.

4: Advice Goes To G7, G8 & G20 Country Top Leaders

It is my honor, I feel proud that I am going to write-up something about G20 country top leaders in this world. If my view goes against you, do not take it by heart, please forgive me.

This is not my intention to hurt you, just criticizing the "decision making mechanism" of your governing system, nothing more than that.

You might say that you are absolutely right in every aspect during your own respective regime, I have nothing to argue with you, but I have some personal views about all of your administration.

For examples,

1. G8 & G20 country top leaders **blaming** each other country and trying to show up their **superpower** or pretending like having everyone has superpower, e.g. **nuclear power**,

2. G8 & G20 country top leaders are **not trusting** each other country and most of the time they goes by,

    ➢ on "skeptical mode",
    ➢ then "on hold",
    ➢ then "on pause",
    ➢ then after high level of communication back and forth among them,
    ➢ then "on running mode",

- ➤ then it goes "trustless, bitter & toxic"
- ➤ The rest of the world becomes victims!
- ➤ Wasting tax payers money i.e. public money
- ➤ What I am trying to say that we have to trust each other and we must have "positive trust attitude mechanism" so that we can feel confident and respect each other.

Another example,

- ❖ Vladimir Putin claims Russia has developed first COVID vaccine (August-2020) which is ready for mankind and it is safe and it has long time immunity,
- ❖ Whitehouse experts were **highly** skeptical on the first news, not only that US official accuses Russia of hacking research,
- ❖ Then Russia dismisses that,
- ❖ Vladimir Putin also claims that one of his daughter has taken it as test basis, she is good in health now,
- ❖ Still skeptical fight started on this issue among them,
- ❖ Wonderful!
- ❖ Carry on "UN Veto Power Country"!
- ❖ I am hopeless!

So as an ordinary general people of this planet I am asking you where should I go?

Who do I trust in this planet?

Whereas UN Veto Power Country (**Russia**) claims something positive for humanity and other Veto Power Country (**USA**) rejects on first news and goes on skeptical mode, it means that **we are on top of fire**.

Very Dangerous Symptoms!!

It is likely as another type of pandemic,

So time to rethink, time to reform the systems,

Please stop it!

3. G8 & G20 country top leaders **threatening** by nuclear test each other country and trying to control each other, but I am trying to say that this is not the way to control this world. We have to change our control policy, time to rethink, time to reform the systems,

4. G8 & G20 country top leaders **imposing sanctions** on the poor countries without justification and United Nations (UN) did not do any actions in this regard, it seems that UN works as if like puppets,

5. G8, G20 and most of the country top leaders, top 250 billionaire and other respective high level officials **stealing** assets by a pen, it becomes a fashion use a pen and steal the property,

UN Veto Power country specially **USA**, **China** and **Russia** not working the way they supposed to work, they are **vindictive** in nature, nowadays **France** started with Turkey.

G7, G8 and G20 country top leaders are not acting positively; they are **vindictive** in nature too,

- Again, you might say that you are 100% correct, I am not arguing with you.

What I am trying to say that as a Leader, do always best thing for mankind, do not follow "autocratic leadership attitude" in the history of World.

- Just imagine momentarily, end of your respective tenure, you will be no longer in position, but people will remember you as an "autocratic-dictator-racist President" in the world history,
- You will be criticized by the rest of the world,
- What will you gain from this regime?
- Absolutely NOTHING!!

I know some of you did some great accomplishments for this world. People will remember that if it is benefited to mankind, no doubt.

So at a glance, the following activities changes rapidly nowadays in this world, it is an alarming rate for all of us, please have a look,

- ➢ Crime rate goes high,
- ➢ Murder rate goes high,
- ➢ Divorce rate goes high,
- ➢ Drinking alcohol rate goes high,
- ➢ Vaping e-cigarette rate goes high,
- ➢ Gambling rate goes high,
- ➢ Gun man misbehave rate goes high,
- ➢ LGBT rate goes high,
- ➢ Environmental pollution making rate goes high,
- ➢ Death in custody rate goes high,
- ➢ Hate rate goes high,
- ➢ The widespread & systemic torture (racism & injustice) of persons in custody by police, security forces and prison guards goes high,

So we are on top of fire, believe me!!!

It is kind of "Public Safety Crisis Globally" has been created by politics by **only** 20 top leaders.

Few Questions Respective Advisors of G20 Countries Top Leaders

- ❖ Mr. Advisor did you ever advice to your President or Prime Minister that Mr. President or Mr. PM that you are doing wrong thing or this idea is not good for the country or your campaign style is not appropriate, people will condemn you at later stage,

If yes, you did a great job for your country and also for this corrupted world,
If not, then why not?

If you did not give him such an advice, then blame will goes to you because you are considered as "key personnel as advisor" of your respective G20 countries every President or Prime Minister.

- Blame will goes to you because you are responsible for advice to the President or PM,
- It means you are failed to motivate to your respective President or PM,
- It means you are sold out somewhere based on my tiny knowledge, I might be wrong or might be correct, let the world reader to comment in this regard,

Why you guys not working properly and make this world peaceful?
What next?
Let's see the next topics "what do we have best solution for this corrupted world" in Chapter 4,

CHAPTER 4

The Best Solution For United States Of America (USA) & Rest Of The World!

In this chapter, I will discuss some sort of solutions for United States of America (USA) where both parties face tremendous abnormal pressure during their 2020 pre-election time. Also I will discuss briefly some solutions for the rest of the world. Please have a look!

I have read many books written by many famous reporters worldwide, many intellectuals, but nobody propose solutions, nobody propose how to solve the current problems in this world, everybody writing up their book 600 pages or 1000 pages and getting best seller award, I do not understand why not writing solutions for G7, G8 and G20 country top leaders who are controlling this world!

The solution I propose here that might be works for you or might not be work but at least my positive efforts are there based on tiny knowledge; the decision is yours, what to do and what not to do. My job is to tell you, the rest is yours.

I am not an expert in analyzing USA election, but I have general feeling as ordinary man based on present abnormal circumstances happening around this USA Election-2020 that's why I am going to write-up here my views for you.

Let's have a look from your inside.

Democratic Party In USA

STEP#1:

The whole world has seen that Democratic Party how much effort they have put on this 2020 election **but in the eyes of Republican Party**, they claim that Democrats are totally incapable to run this country if they win and some other dispute as listed below briefly:

- Democratic Party's agenda are very weak,

- Democratic Party's agenda are "Made in China" based,

- It is very crystal clear that both major parties are **blaming, attacking, insulting, lying, back biting, pressing, pounding, hammering, stealing, hating, dividing and religious cheating** each other, no doubt, the level of blaming and attacking is almost out of control,

- It is something like "rich people" always pressing or pounding on "poor people" what I have seen in South Asia, now watching in North America, wonderful! Make America Great Again!

- It seems to me "Republican party" become rich and pressing and pounding "Democratic Party" and the next "Democratic party" become rich and pressing and pounding "Republican Party" and vice-versa,

STEP#2:

- Democratic Party claim that they are best one and nobody can compete with them and they will make America "Great Again" if they win,

- So they are adamant about this 2020 election and confirm that they will do good things for United States of America and it is 100% clear from their public speech.

- Now what is next?

Republican Party (GOP) In USA

Step#1:

The whole world has seen that Republican Party how much effort they have put on this 2020 election **but in the eyes of Democratic Party**, they claim that Republicans are totally incapable to run this country if they win and some other dispute as listed below briefly:

- Republican Party's agenda are destructive,
- American people are not safe under Republican Party's agenda,

- Under Trump administration, America has become weaker, sicker, poorer and more divided as per Biden,

- It is very crystal clear that both major parties are **blaming, attacking, insulting, lying, back biting, pressing, pounding, hammering, stealing, hating, dividing and religious cheating** each other, no doubt, the level of blaming and attacking is almost out of control,
- It is something like "rich people" always pressing or pounding on "poor people" what I have seen in South Asia, now watching in North America, wonderful! Make America Great Again!
- It seems to me "Republican party" become rich and pressing and pounding "Democratic Party" and the next "Democratic party" become rich and pressing and pounding "Republican Party" and vice-versa,

Step#2:

- Republican Party claim that they are best one and nobody can compete with them if they win and they will make America "Great Again",

- So they are also adamant about this 2020 election and confirm that they will do good things for United States of America and it is 100% clear from their public speech,

- Now what is next?

The Summary From Both Republican & Democratic Parties

The summary from both parties as listed below:

- Both parties are committed to do **good things** for United States of America, it is 100% crystal clear from their public speech,

- Both parties are **attacking** and **blaming** each other and dividing the whole country, it is 100% clear from their public speech,

- Both parties are not on the same page even though they are promised with public that they will do good things if they win, but on different perspectives and dividing the whole country, it is 100% clear from their public speech,

- They are spending **huge amount of money** during pre- election stage. I believe if you add up all money they spent for this 2020-election, you can build a country in South Asia. I guess, total amount would be unbelievable!

- Also both parties are "wasting a lot" in terms of the following:

    - Human energy i.e. work force,
    - Transportation i.e. CO_2 emission,
    - Transportation i.e. Energy based,
    - Financial loss,

Thinking For Best Solutions!

From the above discussions, it is found that both parties want to make America "Great Again"!

Perfect, it is really an excellent idea for all of us.

- If their intention is **really good** to make America "Great Again", then what are the alternate routes are available for them?

- Currently, both parties are in big conflict in the history of American election, they are not on the same page, but both of them are claiming that they will do good things for the country "To Make America Great Again" if they win?

- Currently, they are spending billions over billions dollar to win the 2020-election.

- Currently, they are trying their level best whatever it is (unethical terms like **lying**, **attacking**, insulting, **blaming**, **cheating**, **dividing**, **pounding**) to win the 2020-election.

Then why not to do the following things to get the best results "TO MAKE AMERICA GREAT AGAIN":

- Development plan together to make America Great Again,
- Move together,
- March together,

- United together,
- Talk together,
- Work together,
- Convention together,
- Dinner together,
- To build and make America "Great Again" together

To me this is much easier,

To me this is less costly, **WILL SAVE HUGE AMOUNT OF MONEY**, overall deficit of USA will go down,

To me this is the best route to make America "Great Again" **TOGETHER**

This will make **really** America "Great Again",

This will make **really** hope for this "corrupted world",

The idea is based on "**ALL PARTY GOVERNMENT**"!

What does it mean?

Let's see how does it work?

How Does It Work?

Let's consider only two (2) parties are available in entire United States of America (USA),

For example,

> ➢ Republican Party
>
> ➢ Democratic Party

Each party will be given **269** Electoral College votes by Congress without voting in greater benefit "To Make America Great Again",

They will form "**Coalition Government**" because both of them want to make America "Great Again",

If you listen their national convention talk, every single talk carries the idea that they will "Make America Great Again" based on their capacity,

Then what to do and what will happen?

- Then Justice System will listen their "country development plan" sequentially with deep concentration,

- The Justice System will take "Best Plan" from each party and adopt them in the existing constitution systems as "sub clause" for United States of America,

- Based on that carry on the concept "Make America Great Again" and let the world know how to make America Great Again,

- The rest of the world will **SALUTE** you!

- Current conflict or problem is solved within a minute because both of them want to Make America Great Again,

- This is my feel free opinion as an ordinary man,

- Very simple solution because both parties want to Make America Great Again,

- **All problems, conflicts are solved for USA!**

- Then what will happen?

- Now if USA accepts this very simple solution, then we can think about the whole world,

- What we can do?

- We have to "Reform" all decision making mechanism like UN, IMF, NATO, WORLD BANK, WHO and so on.

- Then what will happen?

Share My Idea With Justice Systems

For example,

If USA Justice systems accept this concept, if it is viable or workable for USA, then the same concept we can through to the rest of the world.

Make a law mandate by G7, G8 and G20 country top leaders with co-operation of International Criminal Court (ICC) and adopt this law worldwide for the greater benefit for mankind to reduce crimes, to reduce personal desire and to reduce abnormal activities from our modern society through United Nations (UN) monitoring,

The individual country must have motivational or awareness team at government level working with modern society explaining them to maintain a safe, reliable and racism free society we must maintain it, nothing wrong with that.

Treat them equally up to Prime Minister (PM) or higher level while giving tickets by the Justice systems.

This is reality, no exception!

This is time to let the world know, how to get rid of all kinds of abnormal activities from our modern society, we must act now before it is already too late and move forward based on that together.

Solutions For USA & Rest Of The World

What we can do now and in future **TOGETHER**?

I would like to request only 20 people in this world including G7, G8 and G20 country top leaders to do the following to avoid global conflicts and unrest:

1. Our G7, G8 and G20 country top leaders must work together globally to prepare a "world class resolution" to ban all kinds of destructive works or hypothesis,

   For examples,

   > Any kind of **Nuclear** test, we do not need nuclear power for this corrupted world because we are so hot tempered in nature and vindictive type, we usually forget about work ethics,

   > Any kind of **Biological Warfare** test, we do not need this type of bio warfare research for this current corrupted world because we are so bad, we are so greedy, we are so untruthful, we always forgot about work ethics,

   > Any kind of **Destructive** research or hypothesis, that leads to negative outcome, just ban on it, we do not need to be "super smart" to make the world environment "toxic, bitter and unpleasant", it is already enough,

This is very important for all of us to avoid global conflicts, unrest and toxic environment. This job must be done by G7, G8 and G20 Country top leaders together from bottom of their heart, because these 20 people are the main culprit in this world.

2. Our G7, G8 and G20 country top leaders must think together globally how to use the following terms to minimize "the global conflict, unrest or crisis":

- "**forgiveness**" such as forgive each other for slight mistakes among the whole world,

- Not applied "might is right or **tit-for-tat**" attitude in every step,

3. Our G7, G8 and G20 country top leaders must **limit only one (1) term for Presidential or Prime Minister ship candidacy** to run an election in Western countries, not more than that and make a law mandate by G7, G8 and G20 country top leaders with co-operation of International Criminal Court (ICC) and adopt this law worldwide for the greater benefit for mankind to reduce crimes, to reduce personal desire and to reduce abnormal activities from our modern society through United Nations (UN) monitoring,

- Every country in this world will follow this law, no exceptions,

- Our main goal is to reduce crimes, to reduce personal desire and to reduce abnormal activities from our modern society;

- We are on top of fire!

4. Our G7, G8 and G20 country top leaders must **limit age level for Presidential or Prime Minister ship candidacy** to run an election in Western countries, not more than 70 years old can run Presidential election and make a law mandate by G7, G8 and G20 country top leaders with co-operation of International Criminal Court (ICC) and adopt this law worldwide for the greater benefit for mankind to reduce crimes, to reduce personal desire and to reduce abnormal activities from our modern society through United Nations (UN) monitoring,

    - Let get in our young stars generation to take over the power and let the intellectuals, experienced people work as "advisory group members",

    - We should be happy in such a manner,

5. Our G7, G8 and G20 country top leaders must **disclose their Tax Returns** without any hesitation, without any further question, there should be time frame given by respective authority like IRS or CRA, if not disclose on time, there would be severe penalty systems for any President or Prime

Minister, no exceptions! Make a law mandate by G7, G8 and G20 country top leaders with co-operation of International Criminal Court (ICC) and adopt this law worldwide for the greater benefit for mankind to reduce crimes, to reduce personal desire and to reduce abnormal activities from our modern society through United Nations (UN) monitoring,

- We are wasting a lot of energy to get tax information for US President, for examples, President's Taxes Chart Chronic Losses, Audit Battle & Income Tax Avoidance (The NY Times),

- Donald Trump paid no income tax in 10 of last 15 years, NY times,
- We are on top of fire,
- We don't have much time to make a drama, we need to cool down this planet, time is very limited,

6. Our G7, G8 and G20 country top leaders must have for every Prime Minister or President of a country **One Spiritual Advisor** so that he can get spiritual counsel in case of necessity based on critical situation occurred, like epidemic, pandemic, disaster etc.,
    - Spiritual leader must advise the president or Prime Minister as per Holy Scriptures with **references** citing what GOD said to follow or what not to follow for this mankind,

- If spiritual leader misguided the President or Prime Minister, then h/she will be punished **severely**,
- And let the world know in this regard of spiritual misguidance,

7. Our G7, G8 and G20 country top leaders must think together globally how to minimize, control, reduce the following negative components from our mind while working in our modern society:

- **Greediness** in terms of excessive desire for wealth,

- **Rehab** drug addicted people, crazy man & women, mentally ill people, and establish moral development in their mindset,

- In our modern society, drug addicted people and dealers, crazy man & women, mental ill people, homeless and street beggar, brainwashed people are around,

- Can you imagine why they have become that type of person in our modern society whereas we have all kinds of modern technology with world class facilities to serve them through our community?

- Why are they become like that?
- Why they become burden of our society?
- Did we ask this question ourselves?
- Did G7, G8 and G20 country top leaders ask this question themselves?

8. Our G7, G8 and G20 country top leaders must **accept the positive criticism** regardless who you are! It is now in very crucial stage for G7, G8 and G20 country top leaders because they are really in very bad shape to lead the world!

    - Think positively instead of all negativity,

    - So make this world peaceful,
    - Make this world lovable,

    - So do not look always for profit,
    - Do not look always for own interest,
    -
    - Please make this world livable for all,
    - You are the main catalyst to poison this world,
    - You are the main culprit to damage this world,

9. Our G7, G8 and G20 country top leaders must have **"trust each other attitude"** in their mindset, especially it is now in very crucial stage for G7, G8 and G20 country top leaders because they do not trust each other and always **skeptical** in nature!

    - If it is not achieved, very difficult to Make America Great Again,
    - **Simultaneously**, If it is not achieved, very difficult to Make This World Great Again,
    - Our intention should be always positive and remain on positive, don't attempt to be negative,

10. Our G7, G8 and G20 country top leaders must **change United Nations (UN) fifteen (15) members Security Council**,

    - The five (5) permanent member countries must have alternate changing policy for every 5 or 10 years if needed based on current demand of the world because current 5 permanent member country they are so egotistic and wild in nature to my personal opinion,
    - They are failed to keep peace, justice, morality for this world!
    - They should be reorganized or reform and put new set of charter or changing policy so that 5 permanent member countries can feel that if necessary then they might lose their positions or membership from UN, in brief, some sort of unseen pressure on them, I am sorry for my comments!

    - The whole world cannot simple rely on 5 UN Veto power countries because they are failed to keep peace for this world!

11. Our G7, G8 and G20 country top leaders must think twice together globally how to remove "**Brainwashing Idea**" from this corrupted world, my personal opinion is that brainwashing idea comes from **50 Richest Billionaire in this world**, therefore, they have significant role on brainwashing general people using creation of business of various types,

For examples,
- Black Friday, Boxing Day, Mother's day/Father's Day and so on,

- People become crazy to buy the products during these days because of their advertisements,

- Limit various digital games, various versions of digital games and so on,

- Stop Online Games to protect our **teenagers**, our young stars generations almost ruined or damaged their life in absence of their mind,

- Our teenagers lost their "moral thinking, do not know respect seniors" because they are super busy with their social media components,

- G7, G8 & G20 country top leaders must be agreed to talk with 50 richest people in this world to stop any kind of production of online games,

- We will lose our young stars generations very soon, probably next 10 years,

- How much **money** our children spending for online games per year worldwide, can you imagine, it is unbelievable! The amount might be touch a "**multi-trillion dollars**" in every 5 years,

- We all must work together to make a success to protect our children, teenagers and some adults too,

- Some teenagers become online game addicted, become abnormal in behavior and attitude too,

- Limit social media usage control such as "You Tubes, Instagram, Facebook, Tik-Tok, Twitter and so on",

- Top 50 richest people they have significant role to change this world. I would say it is better to include up to 250th richest Billionaire. Only these people can change our teenagers to redirect their mindset the way currently they are doing for creation of new business,

- G7, G8 & G20 country top leaders must find some sort of solutions to protect our young stars generations,

12. Our G7, G8 and G20 country top leaders must go through **immediate psychotherapy** required for all highly educated, experienced, and corrupted people worldwide @top level because of the following:

- They are all fabricating, manipulating and lying on their original work assigned by a fountain pen,

- Lying (to tell a lie or modify the original values) is a fashion in our modern society, we must stop lying and mostly done by experienced educated people in our society.
- They are thinking too much to desire of their personal goals,

13. Our G7, G8 and G20 country top leaders must be agreed to maintain that we will not attack any country or any person or any group **based on religion regardless what religion you are holding without proper evidence or reference** because of the following:

    - It creates religious conflicts and makes the environment toxic and bitter,
    - We should respect everybody's religion and create brotherhood relationship and make environment loving each other,
    - It will create peace and justice and fear of God,

14. Our G7, G8 and G20 country top leaders must be agreed to maintain that **if our religious leaders provide wrong information which is conflict with the Holy Book of Bible, Torah and Quran, then there would be severe penalty and ban** the respective religious leaders for the whole life because of the following:

- Christianity-Religious leaders are dividing their Christian people worldwide, they are creating many sects which are conflict with BIBLE to my tiny knowledge and they are busy to full filled their personal goals. They are not coming to a single agreement where all Christians will live in harmony, whereas no divide rules, no deviation, no superiority in the eyes of God. It is out of control now, people are confused where to go and what to do, specially teenagers are blunt in this regard,

- Islam-Religious leaders are dividing their Muslims people worldwide, they are creating many sects which are conflict with Quran to my tiny knowledge, and they are busy to full filled their personal desired or goals. They are not coming to a single agreement where all Muslims will live in harmony, whereas no divide rules, no deviation, no superiority in the eyes of Allah (SWT). It is out of control now, people are confused where to go and what to do, specially teenagers are blunt in this regard,

- Judaism-Religious leaders are dividing their Jewish people worldwide, they are creating many sects which are conflict with Torah to my tiny knowledge, and they are busy to full filled their personal goals. They are not coming to a single agreement where all Jewish will live in harmony, whereas no divide rules, no deviation, no superiority in the eyes of God. It is out of control now, people are confused where to go and what to do, specially teenagers are blunt in this regard,

- Believe in One Holy Book, One Last Prophet and One God, should be all together One Group but they have 1000's of group, why?
- To my tiny views, all religious leaders making different imaginary stories based on human (human-made) and blackmailing human's mind and diverting them and gaining financially. Most of them do not have full time job, they are preaching and gaining money, I might be wrong but based on my research, I found polite cheating in this field, they are not disclosing the main facts based on references with Holy Books.

- Please come forward and do some research on Holy Books given by God to save this humanity by the grace of Almighty God.

15. **Media** is also a **problem** for our modern society.

As of today (August-October, 2020), if you see USA election-2020,
- Media is divided in two (2) main streams,
- Republican media, for example, HANNITY, FOX NEWS they are little bit inclined to Republican,
- Democratic media, for example, CNN, MSNBC they are little bit inclined to Democratic,
- This is a problem for our modern society,
- All news media should work how to MAKE AMERICA GREAT AGAIN , not based on republican and democratic party philosophy,
- Our G7, G8 and G20 country top leaders must think together globally how to control "misuse of print media" in our modern society and make "a world class resolution" that if found print media doing wrong, there would be significant severe penalty for them regardless who you they,
- Media people they know everything (pros and cons i.e. front, back, left, right, top, bottom and inside) of the society,
- They can change this world, they can uncover the truth about this corrupted world,
- But unfortunately some media people are sold out to the business magnates, G20 country top leaders and government and they do not act on what they were supposed to be.

16. As of today, if someone or any group at domestic level or international level do a **crime**,

    - Penalize him/her severely as per local law, disclose the real fact to the public mandatory basis, so that we can learn from this incident,

    - Don't hide the fact/incident for your personal interest and make a trap for that group so that you can blackmail the group and in return selling guns, arms to them and make a critical policy so that they have involved conflict with their own group or country or territory.

    - As a result, your personal goal will be satisfied and you will supply arms to them and the environment would be "toxic, unpleasant and unrest",

    - My personal opinion is that this is mostly done by G7, G8, G20 country top leaders,

    - We must stop it now, otherwise it will be beyond our controls,

17. We must think together globally how to minimize, control, and reduce the desire for **personal goals** at individual level in terms of excessive desire for anything from our mind while working in our modern society.

For examples,
- Poor people or low income people want to become richer,
- Then h/she wants to become a little bit richer,
- Then h/she wants to become one more step richer,
- Then h/she wants to become another step richer,
- Then h/she want to become like a millionaire,
- Then h/she wants to become like a billionaire,
- Then h/she wants to become one of top 50 billionaire in this world,
- Then h/she wants to become 1st richest person like **Jeff Bezos** in this world,

My **first** opinion nothing wrong trying to become the richest person in this world,

But my **second** opinion is about how people are choosing to become rich,

➤ some people involved with crime,
➤ Some people become wild in nature while trying to become rich,
➤ Some people become dishonest,
➤ Some people become liars and smugglers, gangsters,
➤ All are not acceptable paths to become a rich person,
➤ All of these are a problem for our modern society so now what?

That is why I am requesting all including myself that try to become rich in a normal way, not in an abnormal way where our community become corrupted or polluted,

We have to work smart, work hard, solve the problem within short period of time, do not keep the problem intentionally, to make the situation unrest, usually political leaders (**G7, G8 & G20 country top leaders**) keep it to desire their personal goals.

18. Our G7, G8 and G20 country top leaders must think together globally how to control or make a policy "**gun free** modern society" and also how to remove "Gun man" from this community, the society should be gun free!

    - The abnormal usage of gun has many drawbacks, if the person becomes hot tempered for some unknown reason, then if h/she has a gun in his/her home or in hand, then h/she might shoot you in case of high anger,
    - Then what we can do, the incident already happened, nothing we can do,
    - Going to the court, sue him/her and it is long process and wasting tax payers money,
    - The ultimate results, I have lost my loved one!
    - The ultimate results, we have lost my loved one!

19. Our G7, G8 and G20 country top leaders must think together globally how to minimize "**racism out** from our modern society" the world should be racism free society!

- The racism causes many problems; wrong doers must be prosecuted under justice systems and penalize him/her **severely**,
- Let him/her penalize severely so that the rest of the community never think about this, this would be best solution, instead of killing by enforcement officer in public spaces,

For examples,
Black Lives Matters!

George Floyd and Jacob Blake killings stated in Chapter 2 and many more examples also shown in Chapter 2

- Our G7, G8 & G20 country top leaders all need to be **cooperative**, **consistent**, **considerable** and must work together to make a success to save this world as racial free society.
- Our G7, G8 and G20 country top leaders must work together globally how to eradicate all kinds of **systemic injustice stated in chapter 2 from our modern society**, this is very important for all of us to stay in harmony in racism free society now and in future,

20. Our G7, G8 and G20 country top leaders must think together globally how to **eradicate "abnormal thinking from our mind"**,

For examples,

- Hang Fung Gold Technology Group in Hong Kong has a **toilet** worth 29 million dollars,
- Some middle east **Arab Princes**, they have sort of abnormal thinking, all should be eradicate from our mind to save this corrupted world,
- What do you think? Is it worthy to make billions dollars product that has no practical usage for this world?
- It is kind of luxury and wasting money, wasting human brain, wasting everything!
- Outcome is absolutely zero,
- You might say this is my money I will use it as per my wish, yes you are absolutely right but in greater scale it is wasting!
- The ultimate purpose to write up this chapbook is to help to the real needy people in this world and make the world lovely peaceful for everybody,

21. Our **All Book Writers** Worldwide must think carefully at your own capacity while writing a book regardless what types of book you are writing keep in mind how to "**save energy**",

For examples,

> - Prime objective should be tracing the main problems of our modern society and write-up its solutions and disseminate this info to the world readers,
>
> - Please do not increase your book page numbers 1000 pages, 800 pages, 500 pages, do not look for profit all the time,
>
> - It is kind of luxury and wasting money, wasting human brain, wasting everything, wasting papers & labor and ultimately wasting energy worldwide,
>
> - We are on top of fire, we are shortage of energy worldwide,
>
> - You might say this is my money I will use it as per my wish, yes you are absolutely right but in greater scale it is wasting!
>
> - The ultimate purpose to write up this chapbook is to help to the real needy people in this world and it will start helping from your neighborhood and make the world lovely peaceful for everybody,

22. Develop a strong constructive awareness or motivational program **for our G7, G8 and G20 country top leaders and their advisory group peoples** and also for the mass population from government for the following matters:

- Explain about "**usury, legal/illegal income**, bank interests and related activities, this job transfer to "Spiritual Advisor" and he/she will explain to our G7, G8 and G20 country top leaders and their advisory group peoples so that they can understand what is wrong or what is good or what is bad for us,

- Explain Halal/haram income so that ordinary people can understand what is wrong or what is good or what is bad for us,

- Explain Halal/haram foods so that ordinary people can understand what is wrong or what is good or what is bad for us,

- Explain "steal/stealing" income so that ordinary people can understand what is stealing or what is good or what is bad for us,

- To my understanding, many people does not know about this matter, so they have **"do not care attitude"** in this regard, they do whatever they like to do, as a result, crime rate going up, they perform their job without further thinking,

- These jobs has to done quickly otherwise we might get another **pandemic** worldwide because **locust** already in and currently attacking some part of the world,
- These jobs has to done quickly, we have to act now before the earth discharges its burdens [**99:2**],

23. My personal free opinion, you cannot control this "highly educated business oriented corrupted people" in this world in traditional way with highest level of freedom anymore,

- You must change the control policy and again this should be done by G7, G8 and G20 country top leaders,

- My opinion goes to **Justice Systems**, still they can control the G7, G8 and G20 country top leaders giving those warning tickets or full warning tickets through United Nations (UN) if they violate the rules prescribed what they signed for, nobody will argue with justice systems.

- Still the whole world has enough faith on justice systems other than very few in undeveloped countries,

- Our thinking should be reformed and after fine tuning with the existing justice systems, it should be adopted in our modern society of every nation worldwide,

Slogan For 21ˢᵗ Century!

- This is time about change this world by **20 people** only, WHO ARE THEY?
- They are G7, G8 and G20 country top leaders,

- This is time about "**forgive each other**" and build a healthy peaceful, justice based world or nation, WHO CAN BUILD THESE IDEA?
- They are G7, G8 and G20 country top leaders,

- This is time to let the world know that G7, G8 and G20 country top leaders will **promise** from now to on wards, to get rid of all kinds of abnormal activities or conflicts from our modern society,
- We have to act now together before the earth discharges its burdens [**99:2**], so we need to know how to do that and what to do to avoid Global conflict and unrest?

- Top G7, G8 and G20 country top leaders they have significant role to change this world.

- Only these 20 people can change this world safe & reliable racism free world without any hesitation, if they change their mind positively and accepts positive criticism,

This is sort of blended idea and it is about change this world, if you don't believe my idea, I don't have any problem, I can't force you because you are all highly corrupted educated and experienced people worldwide, you have enough sense to understand what is going on around this world.

At the end of the day, think for a minute, what is the benefit to make this world unrest, racial, pushing forward for war?

Think deeply, the final gain would be nothing, today or tomorrow, we all have to die and back to God [**3:185**].

So, I can't say more than that, but at least I tried and called for Global Peace Conference through this chapbook for the G7, G8, and G20 country top world readers so that we can move forward together for best solution to run this world ever and stay safe in racism free society!

God bless you! Ameen.

Call For Global Peace Conference

USA SHOULD CALL FOR GLOBAL PEACE CONFERENCE

USA should call for Global Peace Conference hosted by USA. I wish I will be hosted this conference but I don't have that much capability to reach 7 billion people in this world, that is why I am requesting them.

There would be around two hundred twenty (220) renowned Judges from all over the world will be included in this conference:
- They will listen G20 Leader's opinion,
- They will listen again and again their idea,
- Then the Judges will conclude the final conclusion for this modern society,
- Organizing committee has option to review their final conclusion and decision with Judges.

After reviewing, verifying again with Judges sent it to every country to adopt this mandate on top of their existing justice systems because this is about to change the whole world at this moment to make this corrupted world to reform, reunite to be safe, reliable and racism free.

Make a law mandate by G7, G8 and G20 country top leaders with co-operation of International Criminal Court (ICC) and adopt this law worldwide for the greater benefit for mankind to reduce crimes, to reduce personal desire and to reduce abnormal activities from our modern society through United Nations (UN) monitoring,

Organizing committee must maintain some standards so that each country leader get equal benefits, this would be compiled by one of the committee selected from top G20 countries, as if G20 country top leaders working as "Protector" to protect humanity in this world and working as "Eater" to dismiss everything if you wish, meaning that just eat them, you can break it by violating the rules and regulations,

Let them decide what they (G20) want to do! It is up to them, we are unable to do something as an ordinary people in this planet,

We must be very careful now because we already disturbed this world (if you see Chapter 2 Injustice Happening Around The World page), I believe still we have time to reorganize/reform within ourselves, I personally believe that nobody will argue about this solution if it is comes from justice systems,

Good Luck!

REFERENCES

From Al-Quran

Chapter 3, Surah Aal-e-Imran: 3:185

Chapter 99, Surah Az-Zalzalah: 99:2

From Websites

Based on online search engine,

https://en.wikipedia.org/wiki/George_Floyd
#1: George Floyd Killing! May-2020

Based on online search engine,

https://en.wikipedia.org/wiki/Shooting_of_Jacob_Blake
#2: Jacob Blake Killing! August-2020

Based on online search engine,
https://www.cnn.com/2020/08/31/us/governor-brown-portland-plan-curb-protests/index.html

#3: Portland Killing! August-2020

Based on online search engine,

https://www.cnn.com/2020/06/17/us/man-car-portland-protesters-trnd/index.html

https://au.news.yahoo.com/trump-fans-filmed-driving-through-crowds-and-macing-demonstrators-062145628.html

#4: Drive Through on Crowd in Portland! August-2020

Based on online search engine,

https://en.wikipedia.org/wiki/Stephen_Lecce
Ministry Allocation

Based on online search engine,

https://hyperallergic.com/595372/french-teacher-beheaded-after-showing-muhammad-cartoons-in-class/

https://www.firstpost.com/world/teacher-in-paris-suburb-beheaded-for-discussing-caricatures-of-prophet-muhammad-macron-terms-it-islamist-terrorist-attack-8923511.html
#12 France Teacher Beheaded-How?

Based on online search engine,
https://en.wikipedia.org/wiki/Ravi_Zacharias
MR. PASTOR TO US PRESIDENT,

ABOUT THE AUTHOR

Anayet love to talk about real life events happening around this world. He focuses the current systemic injustice happens every corner of our modern community. He is also thinking why systemic injustice happening and how to solve these problems from our modern society. His intention is to move forward together, for best solution, to live in this world where we can enjoy racism free society in terms of both materialistic and spiritual based life.

His background is electrical engineering and took PhD in electrical systems engineering and taught at university level. Currently he is working in an industry in Ontario. This is Anayet's second book.

You can send your positive criticism from this chapbook mentioning "page number and your main point" to author at the following email:

dranayet2020@gmail.com

GLOSSARY

Democracy-the general meaning of democracy is ruled by the people, government by the people. A form of government in which the supreme power is vested in the people and exercised directly by them or by their elected agents under a free electoral system.

Election-the general meaning of election is how to select or elect a candidate to run a society, city, state, province or a government. An election is a way people can choose their candidate or their preferences in a representative democracy or other form of government.

Materialistic World-excessively concerned with material possessions i.e. money-oriented, who is focused on objects, ownership and wealth. All is money, I need money, I dream money all the time, money is life, life is money, everything is concerned about money.

Spiritual World-relating to religion or religious belief, it indicates to think deeply about hereafter, how we are here and who is created this universe. It is sort of balanced life dealing both this world and hereafter. It does not teach that everything is money-oriented.

Bible-holy scripture of Christianity consisting of the Old and New testaments, revealed on Prophet Isa (Jesus Christ-pbuh) from God

Quran-holy scripture of Muslim people, revealed on Prophet Muhammad (pbuh) from God

Torah-holy scripture of Jewish people, revealed on Prophet Moses (pbuh) from God,

Lightning Source UK Ltd.
Milton Keynes UK
UKHW021851161220
375343UK00008B/465